My Vision in the Mirror

By Mark Postal

"I look my best after an entire hair and makeup team has spent hours perfecting me. When do I feel my best? When I haven't looked in a mirror for days, and I'm doing things that make me happy."

-Anne Hathaway

"Whatever you fear most has no power – it is the fear that has the power."

-Oprah Winfrey

"Sometimes you can't see yourself clearly until you see yourself through the eyes of others."

-Ellen Degeneres

Acknowledgments

I am particularly grateful for a few people's help in the creation of this book. Stacey and Donna, my two counselors in Miami, helped open my eyes to a world I was missing out on. My loving parents paid the ultimate sacrifice and brought me into this world with all of my imperfections. My high school freshman English teacher fielded a request out of the blue to meet with me and help edit my writing. Without him the content of this book would remain unseen, scattered throughout various files on my computer. Thank you for always making me feel as though I was capable of more than my doubting self ever believed.

Contents

Introduction

Who am I? Why is my story worth reading?

I am a 13 year old girl who tries to fit in but feels overweight. I am a 15 year old boy who doesn't feel like he can ever confidently talk to a girl because of his acne. I am an 18 year old girl in college who is too shy to meet people because she feels unattractive. I am a 24 year old guy who would rather stay home on a Friday night than go out with friends because he doesn't like the way he looks. I am someone who doesn't like his body shape, teeth, nose, lips, hair, and skin tone. I am anyone who has ever seriously struggled with accepting their appearance. I am anyone who has ever bought into the notion that life would be significantly better if only they were more attractive. I am anyone who doesn't like seeing pictures of themselves on Facebook. I am anyone whose mood is significantly affected by their appearance. I am a product of television, magazines, movies, advertisements, Facebook, and everything else that shapes my generation's idea of an ideal body image. And I am not alone.

1

Counseling Intake Session

"Today we are going to start with an intake session. I want you to tell me a little bit about what's troubling you. I will then determine how we can help and which counselor will best suit your needs."

Why did they have me meet with a man? I don't want to tell all this stuff to a man. He won't understand. I know I'm male but this is mostly a problem that girls have. He seems so comfortable in his skin. He won't get me.

"Well I think I have something wrong with me. It has been going on since a young age. I think TV and magazines and the media in general are largely responsible. But it's definitely more than that."

"OK. What do you think is wrong with you?"

"I hate the way I look. I always have. I can't stop thinking about my flaws. It's been getting worse and worse. I'm at school here in Miami where everyone is either attractive, confident, or a combination of the two. I'm neither."

I can't tell him about my specific flaws and how I pick apart each and every one incessantly. He'll think I'm crazy. Or he might react in a way that confirms they are noticeable. I can't give him too much more information.

What if he tells people about me? I need him to set me up with a female counselor. She will understand.

" Look, I gotta tell you, I need help. I don't have a lot of time today. I know some people might come in here and just need to talk to someone to get a few pestering problems off their chest. That's not me. I need to see someone as soon as possible."

"Okay, I understand. Do you have any experience with counseling?"

"No. Well I came here once when my girlfriend broke up with me three years ago. Can you set me up with a female counselor? Is that possible?"

"Sure, I should be able to arrange that. You will be getting a call from our office within the next 48 hours."

I walked out of the office into the blazing Miami heat. I had been sweating inside the cool air conditioned office on another beautiful sunny day for everyone else anyway. There was hope. I didn't know if this would help, but it was worth a shot. I thought he was going to say something like "Beauty is only skin deep" and send me on my way. I had heard that cliché hundreds of times in my life, but it didn't help. I wanted to be beautiful on the outside. That was all I cared about. If outward appearance isn't that important why was it all I thought about? I looked at my reflection in each car window as I walked through campus replaying my conversation with him, wondering if he thought I was nuts. I tried to make eye contact with every girl that walked by me on the way to my car. I split time between watching the road and looking at myself in the car mirror while driving home. I pulled up to my dilapidated house and saw my roommates' cars outside. I was happy they were home because I would have people to talk to. I hated being alone with my thoughts then. I walked inside and sat on the couch. The whole back wall had a mirror on it behind the TV and around the fireplace. I sat in front of the fire place so I didn't have to see my reflection.

2

Mirrors

Mirrors are everywhere. I know where each one is in every house, school, and office I have ever spent a considerable amount of time in.

I had a teacher who said something interesting about the mirror. She said, "Everyone must pay homage to it when they walk by. It sort of pulls you in like some magnetic force." I nodded my head in agreement. I always had to look. The mirror truly was my friend and my enemy. I needed to see myself as often as possible. I would sit in my room and look for long periods of time. I would go to the bathroom every chance I had when in public. I could feel perfectly fine, but had to go check that mirror and subject myself to all the emotions that came with it. The urge was so powerful.

I always tried to leave the bathroom on a good note, look at myself from an angle that pleased me so I could leave happy. Most of the time, I didn't even know what I was checking in the first place. Sometimes I would see my reflection and say, "Phew, everything looks OK." Other times I would see my reflection and feel pain- an inescapable feeling that I am stuck with this body for the rest of my life, stuck with this face for the rest of my life, stuck with this skin for the rest of my life. What an overwhelming feeling! I could barely take one day in this body. How would I ever manage to live an entire life in it?

I hated and loved when someone else was washing their hands in the bathroom. I loved that I couldn't look at myself in the mirror to go through the rollercoaster of thoughts and emotions involved in that experience. I couldn't let someone else see me stare at myself. But that was often why I went to the bathroom in the first place- to ride that rollercoaster. I hated that they stood in the way of that.

I would often think how great it must have been to live thousands of years ago before there were mirrors everywhere. What a glorious life it must have been. I noticed I felt much better on days I spent less time looking in the mirror.

 I would try tactics I later learned are called "mirror avoidance" for a whole day. And they worked wonderfully. It's strange how well they worked. Even though I still had all those insecurities in there somewhere, they stayed away from the surface of my thinking when I avoided the mirror. But what kind of life would that be if I never was able to feel comfortable looking at a mirror? I knew I couldn't go on like that forever. More importantly though, I wasn't strong enough to avoid mirrors on a regular basis. Eventually my overwhelming urge to check the mirror at every chance would return. It would start out harmlessly and then turn into longer and more frequent trips. I learned which mirrors had the best lighting, which ones I could usually look at the longest before someone came in, and eventually which ones to avoid altogether because of atrocious lighting, unless of course I felt like subjecting myself to that pain. Sometimes I would go to the mirrors with bad lighting knowing it would bring me down. It was masochistic. What a waste of time and energy I would think in a brief moment of clarity. Clarity was rare.

I liked seeing other people fix themselves up in the mirror. It made me feel less alone. To me it was one's most vulnerable moment. I liked to see someone face to face with the mirror and not think anyone else was paying attention to them. For someone who has been through what I have, it was a strange thing to see another person go through that one on one experience with a mirror. I could see them fixing all the details they felt important to their appearance in the corner of my eye. I felt like I had a sixth sense to notice people that had an increased focus on their own appearance. I suppose spending countless hours thinking about my appearance gave me the ability to notice the tell tale signs. I would pray they didn't have the obsessions I had.

3

Youth

My nose was the first flaw I ever noticed that didn't have an easy fix. The first comment I received was at 9 years old in 3rd grade. A friend of mine had a crush on a girl in our grade and I told him that she had a funny nose. His immediate response to me was, "Yours isn't exactly great either." Ouch. It still stings a little today. Confirmation. It was real. He saw what I saw. My brother and sister made a few jokes about my nose when I was younger but I have a feeling my parents put an end to that. It was enough to make me positive that every person I met saw my abnormal nose, thought about it, and knew it took away from attractiveness.

Two years later my 5th grade class was sitting in the auditorium during lunch. My friend Jackie told me she had a crush on Jonathan Taylor Thomas from a TV show called *Home Improvement*. I was sitting on her right side because I had recently decided my face looked better from that side. I don't know why, but I thought that was my good side and felt much more confident when people were sitting there. Jackie showed me a picture of Jonathan Taylor Thomas in a teen magazine. I had already wanted to look like him. I used to watch his TV show and wish my hair looked like his. We had similar haircuts, but my hair looked nothing like his. He had blonde flowing hair and mine was dark and wavy in an undesirable way. It had already begun. I was 11 years old and jealous of a celebrity.

At my house we had a hair cutting kit with scissors and an electric buzzer. I would sit on a blue step stool on the kitchen floor and my mom would cut my hair trying her best to make it look exactly how I asked. I can still feel the cold buzzer against my head. One time that year I went to school with a new haircut and wasn't sure if I liked it. A girl in my class said she was jealous of me because I had such a cool haircut and she didn't like her hair. It was the best compliment I could have ever gotten. But it wasn't always like this. Usually I would like the haircut for a couple days and then would gradually start to hate it because my hair was frizzy and my head shape was funny. One time my mom cut it too short and I yelled at her. I was so upset. She said it would grow back but she didn't understand. At one point she screwed up so badly I had to shave my entire head. It was terrible. I felt like everyone was staring at me because I looked like a skin head with a funny shaped skull. All I wanted my whole life was to look normal with a very short haircut. Why couldn't I look good with short hair? I had friends who looked normal. I hated them for it. I hated myself for it.

In 6th grade at my older brother's outdoor basketball league, my older sister and her friend told me that people grow into noses after puberty. There was hope. That probably made me feel better than anything I had heard in my life up until that point. Better than any compliment or nice thing anyone ever said to me. I really believed that older people just grew into their noses and mine would eventually look normal. What a comforting feeling.

My parents told me I needed braces at that time. Up until that point my main issues with my attractiveness were my nose, hair, and body. I went through the whole orthodontist process and got my funny looking braces. Shortly after I was playing truth or dare with Jackie from my 5th grade class, on whom I had recently developed a crush. She picked "truth" and said she liked me. I walked home and thought about how she still liked me despite all that metal in my mouth. I remember feeling relieved. This was the beginning of appearance-related thoughts creeping out of my subconscious and into the forefront of my thinking.

In 7th grade at age 13 my elementary school called Orange Avenue merged with a nearby elementary school called Brookside. I had been hanging out with the popular kids from Orange Avenue and my group of friends started hanging out with the popular kids from Brookside. I was immediately attracted to the prettiest girl from Brookside. Everybody had a crush on her. Her name was Jen and I got butterflies in my stomach every time I saw her. She heard I liked her and kids I knew from Brookside set us up. We were downtown sitting outside a TCBY frozen yogurt store and my friend Nick told me to put my arm around her. I did it and felt really awkward the whole time. My palms were sweaty and I was wondering if Jen was attracted to me. The second week Jen and I were dating we went to Nick's on a Friday night. Right before Jen's parents came to take her home, we went into Nick's laundry room and I had my first kiss. We kissed for about 30 seconds and I had no clue if I was doing it right. I went home and felt on top of the world. We talked on the phone the next few nights and Jen started acting strange towards the end of the week. Within a few days she broke up with me. Jen ended up dating an 8th grader who was old for his grade and everyone agreed he was the best looking guy in our school- a big blow to my confidence. I wished I looked like him. He was tall, muscular, athletic, and confident.

Later that year I had a friend over my house and my sister, who was 17 at the time, said, "Your friend is going to be hot when he gets older." Her friends all agreed. I wondered if anyone would ever say that about me. I doubted it. Soon after another girl I dated did call me "hot" in a letter she wrote to me during class. Seeing it written made me feel uncomfortable because I didn't feel like I was. If I was hot Jen wouldn't have dumped me. I knew I wasn't hot. I grew to hate that word as I got older, mainly because of envy towards people who got that label and my growing feeling of being further and further from ever being called it.

The summer between 7th and 8th grade I watched a lot of New York Yankees baseball games. The camera would always show their manager Joe Torre throughout games. He had a really big nose and I would often wonder why he didn't get a nose job to fix it. As a millionaire, he had more than enough money to get the cosmetic procedure. I couldn't understand how someone on TV every night with the money to get a bad nose fixed wouldn't jump at the opportunity. I figured the only explanation was that he didn't want people to know it bothered him. Perhaps he was worried it wouldn't be considered manly for a coach of professional athletes to have cosmetic surgery.

My first memorable experience of feeling it was more than just a few minor things that detracted from my appearance occurred when I was 14 in 8th grade. I had a several friends over my house on a Friday night and wore a maroon polo shirt. A friend told me I looked weird that night, not like myself. I didn't think too much of it. It was winter and my tan was fading. I looked in the mirror when everyone left and agreed I did look different. My features were darker, my skin was lighter and my nose looked worse than usual. I felt ugly for the first time in my life. I walked into the living room and looked at a picture I liked of myself in a soccer uniform taken earlier that year. I thought to myself, "I don't look like that tonight." I now really understood why Jen was dating that older kid and didn't stay with me. Hanging out with popular kids only added to my pressure to feel attractive. I always hung out with the popular kids, but never truly felt like I fit in. Sports were my common thread with them. But I thought popular kids were supposed to be athletic, confident, and attractive, or at least two of the three. I slowly lost my confidence and I certainly lost my feeling of being attractive.

That summer before high school a kid in my grade made a comment about my body and shortly after an older kid at a party said I have my family body shape and nose- just like my siblings. After that I figured they became a pink elephant in the room. Everyone must have known my awkward body and funny nose were there just dominating my appearance, but rarely said anything out of respect, I assumed. Maybe they could see my confidence slowly deteriorating as puberty progressed.

Up until high school I was able to get some attention from girls. I was outgoing and didn't mind being the center of attention at times. Even though I had issues with my appearance that were slowly developing and growing within me, I still was able to present an outward appearance of confidence. Puberty was really what did me in. My skin started changing. I developed acne and went through an awkward growth phase. My body all of the sudden was extremely unappealing. Everything about my looks started to make me feel unattractive.

4

Start of High School

There were two middle schools where I grew up, one on each side of town. After 8th grade we were all combined into one high school and I was excited to make some new friends. On the first day of freshman year I walked around with a group of people on a tour to become acquainted with our new, seemingly massive school. There was a girl in my group that I was attracted to so I tried flirting with her. I later was able to get her phone number and started calling her on weeknights. I helped her with math problems a couple times over the phone. I eventually found out through friends that she wasn't interested in me. That hurt. I was put into the undesirable "friends zone" which I would soon find myself in very often.

I pretty much gave up on trying to get girls to date me for a couple years. I put all my attention into other things like sports and friends. The more I hung out with people of the same sex, the less comfortable I felt around those of the opposite sex. I started to feel anxious whenever I talked to girls. It got to the point where I had so little interaction with females that I would get very nervous when talking to them. I started getting acne at this point and began spending a considerable amount of time in front of the mirror. I could look at myself for upwards of an hour or more. I would watch TV and then during commercials stare at my imperfections for a while. This was the beginning of a struggle that would ultimately leave me feeling defeated throughout high school, college and beyond.

The yearbook used a quote of mine freshman year and needed to take my picture to put next to it. When the yearbook came out I hated the picture. I thought I looked really goofy and hated the fact that everyone in the school was going to see that photo. Its permanence bothered me.

Haircuts only got worse as I got older. During freshman year I got what I felt was a bad haircut. At this point I realized my hair was difficult to cut evenly because of my funny head shape and wavy hair. I was already at the point where I wore a hat between all my classes in the hallways and after school. That previous summer I asked my friends if I looked better with or without a hat. They said I looked better with one but maybe it was because they were used to me wearing it all the time. More confirmation. I was ugly without a hat. The hat actually compounded my problems though because I would get hat hair after wearing it and then my odd skull shape was even more evident during class. This particular haircut in 9th grade was so bad that I asked teachers to allow me to leave my hat on. One teacher wouldn't acquiesce. He insisted that rules are rules. I fought it in front of the whole class and this made me so self conscious. Now everyone in the class would be staring at me. Even worse, they now knew I was unhappy with my appearance and insecure. The teacher told a funny story about a haircut he just had which made me feel a little better. He was going to a wedding and had asked the barber to only cut a little off and to be really careful. The barber screwed up and he showed us all how it was cut unevenly. I wondered how he felt so comfortable showing everyone his bad haircut.

My sophomore year of high school my acne started to get really bad. At this point I really didn't have any interaction with girls at all. I spent countless hours looking at myself in the mirror believing I was absolutely hideous.

I started becoming more and more self conscious about my physique. I never liked my body. Every fitness ad depicted men being big and muscular and women being super skinny and toned. For me the physique I wanted so badly was unattainable. I tried everything to build muscle. It just didn't work. I read a fitness book about gaining muscle mass. It recommended a crazy protein filled diet. I was eating ground beef at 7AM and tuna fish sandwiches at 10 AM for a snack in addition to several more meals throughout the day. I would then lift weights after school for hours. I felt like crap. I tried so hard to achieve a muscular look yet couldn't even tell you why it was so important to me. I started to understand what many girls were going through. The women in magazines were often unhealthily skinny. It was ingrained in our minds to achieve these often unattainable body types. Most people couldn't get their bodies to look like the magazine models in any normal healthy manner. I was told being healthy was really important to feeling good about myself. Unfortunately, my mind was trained to strive for a body that for me could only be achieved in unhealthy ways. I couldn't help but feel like a failure. I already started to hate taking my shirt off in front of other people. Changing in the gym locker room made me feel uncomfortable.

One night I was watching TV and saw a commercial for a plastic surgeon who performed nose jobs in New York. I called the number on the screen and ordered a free pamphlet with information. I got the packet in the mail and looked at "before and after" pictures. I didn't have any money and would never have told my parents that I hated my nose, but became convinced that I would someday have the procedure done. It made me feel better to know something could be done to fix my most dominating flaw.

5

Laura

By junior year, being too insecure to talk to girls really started to bother me. I was 17 and had been single since 8th grade. All I wanted was to be like my sister who was always in a relationship. When she was younger I would hang out with her boyfriend and always admired him. I wanted to have a girlfriend with younger siblings to hang out with that could look up to me. My sister seemed so happy in her relationships. At this point I was becoming resigned to the fact that I probably wouldn't meet a girl until I went away to college. I made a promise to put myself out there if an opportunity came up.

I was on the football team and there was an annual powder puff football game where the junior girls played the senior girls and the football players coached their respective grades. I was nervous coaching because I had to talk to the girls. At the first practice I noticed a girl I had never seen before. It was my third year of high school in a class of roughly 250 people who almost all lived in the same town for 17 years. How was it possible that I had never seen this cute girl? I spent the next couple days asking friends what they knew about her and learned her name was Laura and she was in the Art Club, which met every Wednesday. I had absolutely no connection to her so I decided to join the club. I was really insecure about my acne and pale skin at this time. It was late October and my summer tan had faded. I decided to go tanning at an indoor salon in town. I was so embarrassed and prayed that nobody saw me enter the salon. The owner asked why I was tanning and if I was getting ready for a vacation. I lied and told him that's exactly what I was doing. What a great excuse. People in school started asking why I was tan. I had to lie and say that it must have been from being out in the sun all weekend. Someone at football practice called me a pretty boy. I thought it was the best compliment I had ever received even though it was intended as an insult. Nobody had ever called me a pretty boy in my life. Being considered a pretty boy reaffirmed that tanning was good. I noticed a couple dark spots on my skin after a few tanning sessions and started to fear for my health though. I read online how unhealthy indoor tanning was and this was enough to scare me away. I didn't want to be wrinkly when I got older and get skin cancer. Unfortunately, my issues with tanning would resurface later. I then tried using self tanner. This was before self tanning products were very popular and they still carried a strong odor. I used it one time and missed spots on my neck. People noticed and I quickly stopped that. Thankfully not too many people pointed it out or made fun of me. I just had to hope that the Laura would like me for me and see past my flaws. It was a long shot.

When we first started talking we were chatting online. I was too nervous to talk to her that much in person. She got word from a friend that the only reason I went to Art Club was to meet her. It was so much easier to flirt with her online because I was too insecure to talk in person and it showed in my demeanor. I confessed to her about my tanning and she didn't seem to judge me. After a few days of talking, I asked Laura online to be my girlfriend. She said she would tell me the answer in person. I got to school the next day and she told me yes in the stairwell. I remember being so excited. I couldn't believe that a pretty girl was actually going to give me a chance. The first month I was so nervous that she would see me one day and realize she wasn't attracted to me anymore. As a matter of fact, that feeling never truly went away.

At this point I was becoming increasingly aware of bright lights and their effect on my appearance. I loved hanging out in her basement because the lights were pretty dim. She one time said that she liked sitting on the left side of the couch. I don't know why she said that but I remember being really happy because my left was my good side. On our one month anniversary we went to a Friendly's restaurant. I was terrified. My acne was really bad at this point and we sat right under a bright light. Laura's skin seemed flawless. She didn't have any acne at all. How could she stand looking at me? I was sure that was the last time she would ever date me. It wasn't. She wasn't concerned about my appearance the way I was. Ironically, being able to get a girlfriend, which was my biggest fear in regards to my appearance, often made me more insecure than I was without one. With a girlfriend I felt like I had to constantly look good. I even had to be careful telling her about my insecurities. I heard so much about the importance of confidence when attracting a partner. I didn't want to seem vain, or even worse, insecure. Falling for a girl was great though. I loved sharing life's experiences with her. But I wasn't emotionally ready for a relationship. I had serious issues that I needed to work on.

There was another kid in our school that Laura used to like before we started dating who never showed any interest in her because of her shyness. Once we began dating he started paying attention to her. He asked if she could help tutor him in chemistry. I never thought that I was a jealous person, but this infuriated me. I was terrified of him hanging out with her. He was much more attractive than me. I got so upset that I pleaded with her not to do it. She was a very kind person and couldn't say no. The couple hours that he spent at her house were nerve racking. I was terrified of what could be happening. I didn't think that she would kiss him or anything. I just thought she would realize how much better looking he was. I was going out of my mind that afternoon. It had nothing to do with trust. It had everything to do with my insecurities. After they studied together, we talked on the phone and everything went back to normal. Crisis was averted. Laura didn't leave me for him. I realized how weak I was. I was fortunate that she didn't have much interaction with other guys while we dated, because I was too unstable to handle that.

One day during early January when we had been dating for a few months, she came down with Mono. I asked her if I could stop by because I wanted to tell her something. I got to her house and we sat down on a futon in her basement where we usually hung out. She sat on the left side. I started telling her that I felt very lucky to have met her. Before getting out what I wanted to say I was overcome with emotion. I started crying. I was finally able to get the words out. "I love you." We cried for several minutes. It was an intense experience. I couldn't believe that I had fallen in love. And it was reciprocated! Still, the thoughts about my appearance didn't disappear. I wished more than anything I could be attractive enough to actually deserve her.

I can distinctly remember how I looked during different times of my life and what thoughts I was having about my appearance at each time. During that spring I took the SATs. I went out to eat with Laura right afterwards and sat next to a mirror in a restaurant. I looked at myself several times throughout the meal and hated what I was seeing. I just couldn't get my mind off my appearance. Even on a day where I took a test that could have a huge impact on my future, my appearance was all I was thinking about. She once asked me why I was so unhappy with my looks after I expressed some kind of general complaint. I was too ashamed to tell her

I pretty much hated every single part of my body so I just said it was the acne. She said, "Oh, well that's not permanent. So you just have to realize that it won't always be there." I actually do still have scars years later. But more importantly, everything else I hated was permanent: my body shape, skin, hair, face. There was no way in this lifetime she would ever hear me talk about those flaws. If I mentioned them, she would notice everything she was blinded to and soon lose her attraction towards me. I know she was just trying to help, but I was helpless.

I was in the attendance office at my school one day and a teacher came up to me and said, "What's up with your neck?" I had razor burn and acne all over it. Not one person in the school had said anything since freshman year to my face about it. And a TEACHER commented on it! If he noticed it then everyone must have noticed it. I went to the bathroom afterwards and looked at myself in the mirror for awhile. That was all I thought about for the next week. I asked my brother to take me to the store and buy polo shirts to cover up my neck. The only other time someone said something about my neck acne was freshman year at a party when a random guy asked if I had a disease or hives. I was so embarrassed.

One night that junior year of high school I was hanging out in my friend's basement. I had an older friend who most people considered attractive. My sister's friends saw him at a pre-prom party and said he was hot. It was my second friend they called hot. I now knew I wasn't ever going to be hot. It pained me. This friend saw me without my hat on and said, "You should always wear your hat, you are kind of ugly without a hat on." That stung worse than a punch to the face. I have been stung in South Beach in Miami by a man-o-war jelly fish and it didn't pack any punch compared to the sting of that comment. It still hurts to think about it today- 10 years later. So he said to my face that I am "kind of ugly." That meant he really thought I was hideous and unappealing to the opposite sex. Once something like that was said it couldn't be unsaid. All that was left for me to do was torment myself.

The summer came and I went to the beach with Laura a bunch of times. Despite her constant reassurance, I still felt really uncomfortable taking my shirt off in front of her. She took pictures of us on one trip and later got them developed. I was mortified when I saw myself without a shirt on. I simply couldn't understand how she could see those pictures and continue dating me. She must have known that she could do better than me.

6

Senior Year- Football and Acne

Senior year began and I slowly developed a tiny bit of confidence. I wasn't an underclassmen anymore. I had started to settle into a relationship and felt slightly more secure as a result.   I was elected co-captain of my football team along with my two best childhood friends. We were part of the first winning team at our school in over 25 years. On the surface I had it all. I was captain of the football team with a beautiful girlfriend. Unfortunately my negative thoughts were only beginning. I could barely appreciate anything I had going for me.

One night our football game was televised on my town's local TV network. We won a great game and were all going to a party afterwards. When getting ready, I spent about 15 minutes beating myself up in the mirror. My skin looked particularly pale and my lips were dark red. The contrast between my dark hair and light acne ridden skin made me feel really unattractive. I wondered if people would be judging me at the party. Throughout the rest of the football season Laura would come meet me at the school after our games and greet me coming out of the locker room. I remember feeling nervous that I looked bad while all sweaty and gross. I could never just enjoy a moment for what it was. My mind was never fully there. The winter came and I started feeling really pale and unattractive again.

The acne on my back was now really bad. I tried several different kinds of topical and oral medications and none of them worked. I asked my dermatologist about the most potent medication available. The potential side effects didn't scare me because I was desperate. The medicine was actually very effective, but it really dried my skin out. I was basically shedding and it looked like I had really bad dandruff. Laura didn't mind and would even wipe the dry skin off my shirt. Her not caring obviously made me less self conscious about it. Unfortunately, my back scarred from the acne. I went to a dermatologist that offered laser treatment for scars. I was only 17 years old with no money but needed to know if anything could be done. It was my first time sitting in a doctor's office without an adult. After a consultation the doctor explained that the treatment was painful and might not result in any improvement. The sessions would also cost over $5,000 and insurance didn't cover anything because it was considered cosmetic. I walked to my car with my head down feeling sad that I would have bad scars on my back for the rest of my life. The scars were something I would have trouble dealing with for years to come. It only gave me more desire to keep my shirt on at the beach.

I had a few more really negative experiences with photos throughout the year. Before dating Laura, the only pictures taken of me were at school or sporting events once or twice a year. This was right before digital cameras became mainstream. Laura would use disposable cameras which didn't give you a chance to review and delete pictures you didn't like. I hated my skin tone. I hated my smile. I was slowly developing a hatred for most of the individual characteristics on my body. She showed me the first batch of pictures from a dance we attended and I was disgusted. I could fool her in person with good lighting and my personality, but I couldn't fool her in pictures. Pictures never lie. What a painful experience it was to look at those pictures. She got doubles of every roll and I would take out both copies of the pictures I didn't like and get rid of them. I survived high school by avoiding cameras as much as possible.

7

College Decision

I was going through the whole college application process and was determined to go far away to a warmer place. Two years prior, during my sophomore year, college representatives had come to our gymnasium and set up information tables. I saw a booth for the University of Miami and couldn't believe I had never thought of going there. I spent the entire information session talking to the representative from Miami. I walked out of the gym and declared to my friends that I was going there. I went home and looked in my brother's book of The Best Colleges in America and the University of Miami was in there. That was all I needed to see and subsequently became fixated on this idea. So senior year I sent in an application to University of Miami, but my parents insisted that going to Florida wasn't an option. I also sent applications to Elon University and James Madison University. I liked all the schools, but was dead set on going to Miami. I completed all the applications months early with no help from my parents, which was surprising due to my tendency to procrastinate. I wrote my entrance essay on the topic "Life is too short to be upset all the time." My favorite high school teacher from freshman English helped me. Ironically what he didn't know was that I was always upset. I wanted so badly to live by the philosophy that things out of my control shouldn't upset me, but I was always bothered by my appearance.

I called Miami's admissions office in early January and the woman on the phone told me I should be expecting a package in the mail soon. I yelled, "Package! What does that mean? Does that mean acceptance package??" She laughed and said she couldn't tell me anything except that the correspondence was in the mail. I anxiously checked the mail every day for the next week. I went home one day during lunch, looked in the mailbox, and saw a big envelope from The University of Miami. It had to be good news. They wouldn't send a thick envelope rejecting me. I opened it up and screamed with jubilation. The only other time I can remember screaming like that out of joy with nobody around was when I got my drivers' license and drove away from my house solo for the first time. I called my mom and she started crying on the other end of phone. My parents were still against my going there. I asked if she was crying out of joy or sadness. She said, "I don't know, happiness." She knew how important it was to me. I had even applied to another small school in Florida which I knew nothing about while I was waiting to hear from Miami. I visited the University of Miami with my parents in March. We looked around the campus and it was love at first sight. I sat in on an interesting Business Law class and became really excited for stimulating college level courses. We went to South Beach and walked around this beautiful vacation destination located only 20 minutes from campus. I was eager to make South Florida my new home. It would be a new start on life.

When I got back home I looked at some pictures my mom took on her digital camera in Miami. We took one on the beach where I looked really pale compared to all the tan beachgoers. I felt so ugly in those pictures. I should have known this was a sign of times to come. I convinced my parents to let me go to school there after the trip. Words can't describe my excitement the moment they acquiesced.

I was back to reality in New Jersey after our visit. Laura's best friend from childhood had moved away when they were much younger, but they still kept in touch. She told her long distance friend about me on several occasions. Laura once sent her a picture on the computer and said, "It doesn't do him justice." That was the first indication that Laura was blinded to my flaws. That picture did me justice. It showed exactly how ugly I was. We had been dating for over a year and this friend was coming to visit that spring. Naturally, Laura wanted me to meet her. My acne scars were really bad on my neck at this point. I decided I would meet her but I had to wear a shirt that would cover my neck. I didn't care that I looked dorky in the collared shirt. I couldn't risk her friend seeing the scars and telling Laura how bad they actually were. Laura would then figure out she is better looking than me and could get a more attractive boyfriend. Her friend visited, we all had a good time, and Laura told me that I was well received. I was relieved to survive that experience. I felt stupid for worrying so much.

Laura would often tell me that I was really cute or handsome. Sometimes it was nice to hear that. Other times I was just thinking about how her eyes would eventually be opened to how ugly I really was. She would occasionally talk about how annoying her ex-boyfriends were. She would mention how they weren't really attractive and didn't know what she ever saw in them. I once said, "I don't ever expect us to break up, but if we do, do you think you'll feel the same way about me? That I'm not really attractive and you were just blinded by love." She said, "Definitely not, because you really are an attractive guy. My friends think you are too." I wanted to believe her, but I just couldn't. I was certain she would look at pictures of me and notice all of my flaws. She would think how happy she was that she didn't stay with me. She would realize we would have had ugly children. I hated believing this. I would rather her wonder how she ever fell in love with my personality and hate everything about me as a person, but still believe that I was attractive. I figured people can change their personalities a lot easier than their looks. That's how screwed up my thoughts were.

 Despite all of my struggles, the school year was flying by. Before I knew it senior year was winding down and the prom was approaching. I became nervous because I knew everyone was going to be dressed up and looking their best. My best was still ugly. I would have to take tons of pictures with Laura and would look really unattractive next to her. I managed to get through the whole prom, but was becoming increasingly uncomfortable in my own skin. I felt sorry for myself all the time. My school held a function called "project graduation" after our graduation ceremony and the venue had a pool. I went swimming and had to take my shirt off. I felt really uncomfortable half naked and tried to stay far away from my classmates. They were all having fun playing games in the water and I couldn't enjoy myself. I got out after a few minutes. I said bye to some friends at the end of the night. I told one kid I really liked that it was sad because we were good friends in school but would probably never see each other again. We had a kind of sad goodbye and I have never seen him to this day. It was sad moving on and never seeing certain people again.

The summer after senior year was short for me. I had to say goodbye to my girlfriend, my first love. Laura was staying in New Jersey for college so we would be entering a long distance relationship. We had no idea how things were going to change long distance. She had mentioned to me in the spring that she thought we should be in an "open relationship" so there wasn't too much pressure at school. She said the intention would be to stay together, but we wouldn't have to feel tied down or really guilty if we were meeting and talking to new people. I agreed with her. I later found out that she wanted this status because she was scared I would talk to girls and then feel like I had to break up with her out of guilt. She had no intentions of meeting a new guy. I left for school a month before her and during that time I was perfectly fine with the "open" arrangement. As soon as she arrived at her school a thousand miles away, she went out the first night with some people from her dorm. We were on the phone and I overheard a guy that approached her. I then heard her say, "Sorry, I have a boyfriend." I couldn't sleep that night. The thought of guys approaching her was terrifying. The first thing in the morning I told her I didn't want to be in an open relationship anymore. She was willing to remove that status and go back to being totally exclusive. I felt relieved.

8

Arrival at College

I had arrived at the University of Miami in early August. When I got there I wondered why I chose to go to a school in South Florida where people couldn't hide their bodies in hooded sweatshirts and jeans. Sure, it is actually a great school academically, but most students I met didn't fit the stereotypical geeky definition of an academic. These kids were smart, confident, and socially adept. At first, I didn't realize the extent of my insecurities when I went away to school. I hoped I was just going through an awkward phase that I would mature out of. And that probably was true *partially*. But that phase lasted a lot longer than I anticipated. I now also believe part of it is a lot deeper than that.

I used my athletic ability and friendship with a couple of other people to circumvent the normal bid selection process and so was able to join the most difficult fraternity to receive a bid from. I would have never survived formal interviews with the older members. The confidence in their demeanor and questions would have eaten me alive. I was now in the supposed jock fraternity which turned out to be a big mistake. There was a day that every new fraternity and sorority pledge on campus got their bids in front of each other. It was a sunny Miami afternoon and we were in the middle of campus lined up with our new pledge class. I looked around and probably never felt more out of place in my life. I hadn't made friends with any of them yet. They were all better looking, more confident and secure and seemed to feel like they belonged. We didn't have any bad hazing, but one time they had us close our eyes in a hallway and they put a haircutting buzzer up to my ear joking that they'd shave my curly locks off. I remember thinking if that buzzer touched my head I would stand up and drop out of the fraternity in a heartbeat. I wasn't going to shave my head for anything. Fortunately they were just messing with us. During the pledging process one brother said I always seemed scared and nervous in front of everyone. He saw how weak I was. Shortly after getting initiated I got in a wrestling match one night with another brother in our house. I don't know why we decided to fight. We didn't hate each other or anything. We just decided it was a good idea to wrestle with everyone watching. I remember the feeling after we both put up a good fight and gave each other some good shots. I enjoyed seeing the older brother, who no longer saw me as weak or scared, talking about the fight. The wrestling match was my attempt to fit into a place where I didn't belong. We had dances and other events with sorority girls on campus. I was so awkward in conversation. I usually tried to find another guy who didn't seem to be talking to girls and would hang out with him at the events. Most of my friends weren't in my fraternity because I really just didn't feel comfortable socializing with those guys. We were opposites in so many ways.

Around this time there was a TV show on MTV called *Diary* which followed celebrities during their everyday lives. The introduction to the show started with the line "You think you know, but you have no idea." That's how I felt about other people interacting with me. Some people thought they knew me, but they really had no idea. People at home saw me as the popular guy with the pretty girlfriend who played football and got to attend school in Florida at the University of Miami. The kids I met at school saw me as the guy in Pike, the jock fraternity. They all had no idea what thoughts were inside my head. Nobody knew that I was such a negative person who hated so much about himself. I tried so hard to project this image of being happy and worry free.

I tried to gain some confidence by performing well in school but had a lot of trouble focusing during that first semester. One lecture however did really catch my attention. My psychology teacher mentioned that a growing body of research existed suggesting that good looking people were more likely to succeed in our society. Findings indicated that people who were perceived as better looking were more likely to be considered smart, happy, and talented. I now believed that good looking people were more likely to be successful and realized my life was going to be that much harder.

The professor also mentioned that women's confidence tended to be more affected by their perception of their appearance than their male counterparts. He explained that society seemed to place more importance on looks for women while men were expected to gain more self-worth from status. I remember believing that trend was gradually changing. For me, there was a lot of pressure to look good as a male. The traditional role of thinking that man's confidence was more correlated with status than perception of his appearance may have held true to a large extent as a typical man got older and advanced his career in the workplace. However, in middle school, high school, throughout college, and even early years of work there didn't seem to be many males with roles of distinguishable status. One thing I knew for sure was that society's obsession with appearance had slowly but surely crept into my personal framework for confidence.

Since I didn't really feel comfortable around the kids in my fraternity I spent most of my free time with kids on my dorm floor. My roommate was a really nice guy named Jim from Key Largo, Florida. He was into water sports and grew up on the water. Our hobbies were very different but we made a connection early on and his sister said we were perfect for each other. We were both silly and constantly joking around. There were some other great guys on our floor as well. Memo, short for Mehmet, was from Istanbul, Turkey and had a memorable accent. He was the most energetic person I ever met and was friends with everyone on campus. Memo always made sure people were having fun. Another guy was Nick from Germany. He was actually from Denmark, but his name tag on his door said German Nick because that's where his family lived most recently. He was a more reserved guy, but was really nice. I was jealous of his Scandanavian looks with his blonde hair and blue eyes. Nick's roommate Jason was another fun guy who I convinced to join my fraternity. Pravin was my other really close friend. He was from Chicago and his whole family was from Sri Lanka, a small tiny island nation south of India which I didn't even know existed until I met him. When he told me stories about his visits to Sri Lanka I would wish I could live in a place like that where most people worried only about basic needs. Having all my basic needs taken care of in America like food, clothing and safety, left me with too much time to think about everything else I wanted, like a perfect face and body. Pravin was a superb athlete and we bonded over our love of sports. I was very fortunate to meet all these great guys my freshman year.

Despite meeting all these quality people, I spent way too much time talking to Laura during my first semester away. I went to some other non-fraternity parties and social functions with my dorm friends but continually felt awkward whenever I met girls. This reaffirmed that I would never be able to meet anyone else. I went to visit Laura after being apart for almost two months. I was so nervous going up there and decided to surprise her. I told her I was coming within the next few weeks and didn't want her to know which weekend it would be. I was scared that her friends wouldn't think I was attractive when I arrived and I hoped traveling a 1,000 miles to surprise her would make me seem like a worthy boyfriend. I feared they would all tell her she could do better than me. I again survived this trip but I was growing increasingly nervous about our relationship. I didn't have a great first semester with friends because of all the time I spent talking to her. It was comforting to talk to her. I felt less insecure when we talked and didn't have to go out and meet new people.

She then visited me in Miami in November and I remember being upset about a minor acne breakout. I wondered if she would still be attracted to me after seeing all the other options at her college. Laura was someone who I dated for two years at this point yet I still had these thoughts. Sometimes being in a relationship quieted the appearance thoughts because I didn't feel like I had to look good for every potential suitor I met. Other times it made the thoughts much worse when I didn't feel good enough for her.

I would often eat alone in the school cafeteria looking at other people who seemed happier. Students who had problems, but not my problems, conversed within an earshot. They talked about grades, displeasure with the plot of last night's episode of a TV show, or an annoying roommate or teacher. I sat there and wished those were my problems. I wanted normal problems. I'd get up and go to the bathroom which had horrible lighting and see how everything looked. I knew this one had particularly bright lighting so the results were already predictable. I felt dejected in there. I walked out and got more food from the buffet. The food was comforting. The woman serving my food would smile and seem cheery for no particular reason. Her name was Hazel. Everyone knew Hazel because she was so uplifting. She gave me hope. I would have hated to serve food to kids at a college who didn't seem like they appreciated it, but she just seemed happy. She appeared content with her life. I wondered how many people Hazel made smile in a day. Her values were better than mine. Her source of self-worth was better than mine. She had something I wanted and I needed to figure out how to get it. It was a contagious appreciation for life.

I went home for winter break and felt relieved to be around my family and girlfriend again. It was a safe place for me compared to Miami. Without any roots in Florida I often felt like a lost soul.

9

Heartbreak

I returned back to school in January and was in for the surprise of a lifetime. Laura called one day and said she wanted to talk. She had uttered those dreaded words no person in a relationship ever wants to hear. She then told me that she wanted to go back to being in an open relationship which I translated as her wanting to see other people.

Although the distance and other factors had taken their toll on our relationship, her call came as a complete shock to me. My friends back home were shocked because I projected an image of a confident person to them and of having the proverbial upper-hand in the relationship. Nobody thought she would ever be the one to end it. I had such strong feelings for Laura and couldn't bear the thought of losing her. Naturally, being the incredibly insecure person I was, I smothered her and pushed her away when she told me this.

I kept calling her several times a day. She accidentally picked up the phone one time and didn't realize I could hear her. "It's Mark. I don't want to talk to him now," I heard from a distance. She then hung up. I called back again and again with no answer. I cried. I balled my eyes out. It was the most painful experience I could ever imagine. I couldn't believe that my body didn't run out of tears, they just kept pouring down my face.

The phone conversation that officially ended the relationship took place while I sat in a chair on the intramural field in front of my dorm. Laura again said she needed to talk and I knew what she was going to say. She told me to go out and meet other people- easy for her to say. I walked back into the dorm broken. I was being held up by someone a thousand miles away. I was a faulty structure and she was sturdy. The moment that phone call ended, my frail structure had to stand on its own.

Jim made me go out to a party that night. I ran into a girl I knew and yelled into her ear over the loud music, "My girlfriend broke up with me tonight." That was my pickup line. I wasn't looking to meet anyone new though. The only thing I needed was someone to lean on. Over the next three months I endured heart piercing pain. I had to deal with losing my first love, which is a full time job in itself. On top of that I had to face a campus full of seemingly secure girls and guys. The mirror became my obsession. The thoughts about my appearance took over. I wondered how anyone would ever find me attractive again. I tricked Laura. Somehow she was able to see past my physical flaws. I don't know how, but she did. I would never find someone like her.

I called my sister several times over the next few weeks and called girls that were friends back home. I called my mom. I reached out to anyone that would listen. I was a wreck and being heartbroken was intense. My mom told me that having your heart broken can almost be like a death in some ways, and that's tough because the person is still there which can make closure very difficult. I understood what she was saying.

Before the breakup, I had already booked a flight to see Laura in February. I stayed after my psychology class and asked the teacher what he thought I should do. I can't remember exactly what he said, but it was something to the effect that if I didn't go I might always wonder if I could have salvaged it. He might not have even said that, but it's what I wanted to hear. I decided to go. It was so hard being with her that time because I still felt like we were dating. I wanted to hold her hand, but she didn't want to hold mine. I met a guy named Pat that I suspected she was interested in. He was taller and much better looking than me. I started questioning her about Pat. She finally admitted that she was in fact curious about him. She had told me if I hadn't forced her to take away our status as an "open relationship" as originally planned, she wouldn't have felt so guilty talking to another guy. I realized my insecurity was to blame for our breakup. This was very difficult to swallow. We had kissed at one point during the trip and she started crying afterwards. I realized what I was putting her through. She didn't want me to be there, she wanted space. I left there feeling a mix of happiness and sadness- but very empty overall.

Valentine's Day was about a week after that visit. I had been feeling fine early in the day. I then went to the beach with Jim and saw other couples hanging out. It was so hard to see happy people together. Suddenly all the sappy songs on the radio were making so much sense. It was like every song about breaking up was written specifically for me. I would never find a girl like my ex-girlfriend. No pretty girl would ever be attracted to me. I looked at my phone and saw a missed call from Laura. Jim knew how much I was struggling and convinced me not to call her back right away. I talked to her later and realized she was just lonely on Valentine's Day. It wasn't about me.

The next big decision was spring break. Laura and I had been talking a little since my visit to her. Before the breakup, I had also purchased her a flight for spring break to visit Miami. I could tell she really didn't want to come. I basically gave her an ultimatum that I would never talk to her again if she didn't come. I didn't say that I would kill myself, but implied my life wasn't worth living without her in it. I don't know if I thought this desperation would help win her back. Obviously it wouldn't, it was just scaring her. She was truly conflicted, but finally reluctantly decided to come. I was thrilled. We hung out all week and went up to a friend's house near Orlando for a few days. I felt like we were dating again even though she made it clear we weren't. When a girl I had been friends with called during the trip, Laura saw the name pop up on my caller ID and seemed to get a little jealous. I was really happy she saw that. I didn't know where we stood at the end of the trip.

After Laura left, I hung out one night with an older member of my fraternity who everyone had sought advice from. He was a genuinely nice guy. I told him that I was devastated about losing her and had been so sure we were going to get married. He told me that everyone thinks that about their first love. He told me he thought that about his first relationship and has had many since then. I figured he just didn't understand. Laura had to be the one.

Finally, one night during that second semester after her telling me yet again that we weren't together when I implied we still were, I decided the only way to move on was to completely cut off ties. I told her I couldn't talk to her anymore. We stopped talking and I started moving on. It was very difficult being single. The thoughts about my appearance were intense. I spent a lot of time looking in the bathroom mirror on my dorm floor. I removed all of our connections to each other on the internet so I wouldn't be tempted to check up on her. I tried hard to distract myself with school. After about a month of giving her space I finally succumbed and checked her profile. She had lyrics about regret from a song called *The Reason* by Hoobastank.

She must have been talking about me. I decided to contact her. She apologized for everything and we decided to get back together when I was coming home next week for summer. We dated for the next year and a half but my heart was never fully in it. Once I had been heartbroken I became extremely guarded. I couldn't go through that experience again. I wasn't strong enough to endure that. But the damage to my psyche was done. I now knew how terrifying it was to be single in Miami.

10

Fraternity Life

Sophomore year of college I was really excited to come back to school because I was moving into my fraternity house with a pool in our front yard. My brother lived in a frat house at Lehigh University in Pennsylvania for three years and it seemed like a blast every time I visited. Within the first few weeks I tried hanging out with the fraternity members, but I just didn't fit in. One day we went swimming at South Beach because a hurricane off the coast produced some great waves. All the other guys were muscular and tan. I figured they judged me for my appearance and thought I wasn't cool because I was much less attractive than them. I never lied out at our pool even once with my shirt off after realizing how my body looked compared to theirs.

One day we were sitting in someone's room talking about whether or not particular girls we knew were attractive. I used to talk about people's flaws out loud when discussing whether or not they were good looking. As I got older I tried so hard to not mention any flaw of another person. I knew what it would feel like to have someone say that about me. I often wondered what people talked about when my name came up in a 'hot or not' conversation. I wondered what sorority girls talking about me would say. I thought having to listen to that conversation would have been worse than physical torture. I would have hated hearing people provide reasons why I am unattractive, having to hear each and every feature dissected. I kept my mouth shut during the conversation and just listened.

That experience made me think what it would be like to hear other's thoughts as they looked at me. Friends, girls, people passing by- what did they all think about my appearance when they analyzed me? I decided that would be the worst super power to have. To hear the compliments and nice thoughts would be great, but the inevitable criticisms and confirmation of my flaws would be unbearable. "Oh, what an unfortunate body." "I'm glad I don't have his skin." "I can get a better looking guy than him, right?" "I'm glad I don't have a face like that, poor guy." These are all things they must have been saying. The worst would be something like, "There's nothing in particular that stands out as wrong, but he's just not an attractive person."

I rarely hung out with the fraternity guys the rest of the year. My only other friend in a fraternity was my roommate from freshman year, Jim. All of my other good friends from my floor freshman year moved into an upperclassmen floor in a dorm on campus. I often wished I had moved into the dorms with them. They were my genuine, sincere, non-judgmental friends. I don't know if the fraternity guys were really judgmental or if it was just my insecurity that prevented me from bonding with them. I spent much of that year sleeping in late and locking myself in my room at the end of the hall. We had community showers that I always rushed in and out of hoping nobody would see my body in a towel walking down the hallway. The only thing that made me feel good that year was playing basketball at the Wellness Center across the street.

I used to play a lot of basketball at that gym. The multimillion dollar gym on our campus had huge windows with sun beaming in and palm trees in the main hallway. It was my favorite place on campus. I enjoyed playing sports my entire life. Only once in a while would I wonder if people thought I was ugly when I played. My face would turn bright red by the end of a session and I hated the way I looked in the mirror. I would sometimes stop to buy a sports drink afterwards and have trouble making eye contact with the store clerk because I felt so ugly. But, believe it or not, even though I felt more unattractive at the end of a hard cardio session, I actually felt great overall. The endorphin rush outweighed the increased perception of ugliness. It wasn't about looks when I was playing basketball. I wasn't being judged by my appearance on the court. I was being judged on how good of a teammate I was and how hard I worked. I ran so hard that it didn't even matter how well I played. I had a runner's high every time I walked out of the gym. That court was a refuge for me. No mirrors. I could avoid the mirrors in the gym while lifting weights and using the machines, but that wasn't even an issue on the basketball court. It became clear to me that this would have to be incorporated into my strategy of decreasing the importance of my appearance with regards to my self esteem. It wasn't so much that I felt I looked much better while fit, because on many levels I still hated almost everything about my appearance. The benefit was from feeling like I was treating my body right and actually being healthy. Unfortunately I would often stray away from exercise.

I must admit, the gym wasn't all pleasant though. Sometimes it seemed like a place where really good looking people decided to gather and show off their attractiveness. I would look around the gym wishing I had different body parts of people. I wanted that body, with that hair, those lips, and that smile. I would do this in class too. It wasn't just the gym, but it seemed more common there. I also would check out girls and feel like they weren't interested in me. I would see them looking at other guys. I would try to make eye contact with them and see if they smiled or would look away. These were all things I had to work on because I knew working out and at least feeling healthy regardless of my actual appearance was going to be crucial if I wanted any normalcy with my thoughts. Having a workout partner helped a lot because I could talk to him instead of getting deep into my own unpleasant thoughts. I also tried working out late at night or at odd hours when the gym wouldn't be crowded so I could get more confident being in that environment.

My family came down to visit me that February. I met them at the airport and they all looked so pale. I couldn't believe that my skin normally looked like theirs. I imagined how much worse it would be if I was pale. From that point on I became convinced that I would never be able to live anywhere that wasn't warm and sunny all year round. The only way I could live up in the north again was if I used self tanner every day or went back to the tanning salons and I didn't want to do that. I was depressed thinking that I would never be able to live near my family again. Most of the time I convinced myself the reason I wanted to stay in warm weather away from my family was because I hated the cold, but the fear of being uglier was so much stronger than any other fear I could have. Then I would have battles in my head thinking that it would be so much easier to live in the north where everyone wore sweatshirts and jeans for most of the year. I wouldn't have to worry about taking my shirt off at the beach. We could all hang out inside in the cold weather. I came to the conclusion that I was damned no matter where I lived. I would be ugly in the south and ugly in the north.

My freshman year of college only a few pictures were taken of me. Sophomore year things were about to change in a big way. One fraternity brother started telling me about a new website called Facebook. I was told it was sort of like MySpace but only college students could join. I immediately knew this website could change everything about my social life. Digital cameras had now become mainstream and people took them everywhere. People could upload their digital pictures on the internet and make them appear on my personal Facebook page to be viewed by all of my friends. Now everyone would be able to see all my imperfections on the internet whenever they chose to. I could make it so people wouldn't see the picture on my personal page by "untagging" it, but if they saw my friend's pictures they would still see me. It was basically unavoidable. A picture is permanent. I couldn't ask people to take them down because the only thing worse than feeling bad about my appearance was having people know I felt bad about it. I was 19 years old and Facebook had changed the landscape of my life. It became evident to me at this point that I would either entirely avoid social situations which basically all had cameras or I would have to change my thinking drastically. But how? I had no clue how to do that. I kind of felt trapped with this mindset for the rest of my life. It had been several years at this point since the self defeating thoughts started and things were getting progressively worse.

In many ways I consider this a lost year of my life. I did really poorly in school and was distant from everyone around me. My fraternity had gotten in some trouble with the school for parties and our headquarters proactively kicked everyone out and made us all reapply for membership. They wanted to weed out the trouble makers. I decided there was no point in reapplying because we were told that due to a fire code violation we couldn't live in the house next year. It turned out to be the best thing that ever happened to me because Memo, Nick, and Pravin asked me and Jim to sign a lease to live in an off campus house the upcoming year. The fraternity house kind of turned into a dump the last month we lived there because everyone was upset we couldn't live there the next year. I was relieved when the school year ended and couldn't wait to go back home to New Jersey.

I came home from college that summer sporting a good tan with my hair grown out and bleached blonde. Everyone at school thought I had natural blonde hair, but I had been using products to dye it all along. A girl in my town told me that college made me hot. It was only the second time I was called hot in my life. This was further evidence I had to stay tan now. I didn't care about the health effects anymore. Looking as good as I possibly could was all I cared about now. That summer flew by and I was excited to move in with my good friends upon my return.

11

Café Tu Tu Tango

When I got back to Miami in the fall of 2005 I needed to find a job to earn some spending money. My friends and I were all turning 21 this year and we would need money to go out to bars and clubs. I decided to look for work at a restaurant in Coconut Grove, which was not too far from my campus. I got hired at a place called Café Tu Tu Tango that served tapas style dishes where everyone in a dinner party shared the food. It was a fast and vibrant atmosphere that had tango dancers on some nights dancing throughout the restaurant. Once a night shift began there wasn't much time to think about anything except remembering orders and hustling from one table to the next. What a great feeling to have six or seven hours to escape from the mental prison I now lived in. This work really helped take my mind off of my appearance. Occasionally I would go to the bathroom, check the mirror and feel dejected for a moment, but was usually able to get right back on the floor and forget all that nonsense. I was able to use my personality to joke around with people without feeling too self conscious. For some reason that chaotic environment was the perfect recipe to escape it all. I wasn't dealing with my issues per se- they would all be there when I went home. The negative thoughts would still persist when I was stuck in the library with a couple books and a bunch of normal looking people. I did get my first taste of feeling satisfaction from work though. I wasn't saving the world with my job or changing people's lives like I dreamt of in school. But I was getting my hands dirty and taking a little pride in a job that had to be done. It actually did increase my self esteem quite a bit. This was my first hint that devotion to a job could be a source of breaking the tie of self-worth to the perception of my appearance.

 Surprisingly, I even started to smile again occasionally. I had grown to hate my smile throughout college. I started to feel happy at times while working. This feeling was unusual as of late because I was getting deeper and darker in my head with the negative appearance thoughts. There was a chef at Tu Tu Tango who clearly could have used braces on his teeth. His front teeth were all over the place but he smiled often. I remember thinking I would never be able to smile if I had his teeth. His smile was incredible though. It was a smile of confidence, one of genuine happiness. When he smiled I could tell he simply did not care that his teeth were crooked. He had something I wanted. The negative part of my brain said he was just oblivious. I figured no one had ever made him aware that his smile wasn't what the magazine models had. His smile wasn't what my parents, orthodontist, and society told me was necessary to be content with. In reality, he probably did occasionally desire straighter teeth. But he didn't care the way I did. His self esteem was tied to healthier things- perhaps his morals, his love for his family and friends, or his ability to work hard and produce a good meal for hungry people.

One day after work, when feeling very lonely, I decided to go to another restaurant down the block. I sat down and ordered something to eat. I looked out on the dance floor and saw a dorky guy dancing. The song "Blister in the Sun" by the Violent Femmes began playing. The dorky guy started dancing wildly like he didn't have a care in the world. He seemed to be dancing with friends. I was jealous of him. I always wanted to dance but was too self conscious to. Could I ever be like that? Could I ever go out there and just move around like nobody was watching?

****

When I first got hired at Café Tu Tu Tango my manager, Michael, had us do a one minute exercise during training. Each new server had to stand on top of a chair for 60 seconds and talk about themselves. Many people ran out of things to say after 40 seconds. The point of the exercise was to show us how long 60 seconds can feel when customers are waiting to be served. One person who spoke was a very good looking guy. His name was Bart Grzybowski. He spoke about how his job at the restaurant was a second job for him. Bart had just moved to Miami from up north and was working full time for a religiously affiliated volunteer organization with refugee children from mostly Hispanic countries. He seemed so confident. I wasn't really sure what to make of him. He seemed like a nice guy when we had a few brief conversations over the next couple of weeks, but I wasn't trying to make any new friends at work.

A few weeks into the job I flew home for a wedding. My trip ended up being extended 10 days because Hurricane Wilma struck Miami while I was gone. There was no power at my house or the restaurant for over a week in Miami. The airline was kind enough to extend my flight without a charge. While staying in New Jersey I got a call from Bart asking me to hang out. I thought it was strange because I didn't really know him but figured he was trying to make friends. When I got back to Miami we started hanging out. Bart spoke of tragedy he had experienced in his life. His mother died far too young while he was still in high school. The untimely death led him to want to make a difference in the world which is why he was volunteering with refugee kids. I immediately drew a lot of inspiration from him. I was stuck with my miserable existence from entirely self created thoughts and beliefs. Bart, on the other hand, was dealt a tough hand in life. His mother was suddenly taken away from him. He had no control over his loss. It didn't matter how attractive he was. Girls literally would walk up to him, hand over their phone number on a piece of paper, and walk away. I had never seen anything like that before. But no matter how good looking he was it didn't change the fact that he was brought to near suicidal thoughts after losing his mother. In another short-lived moment of clarity, I thought, "That's what matters most. Family, friends, love- not looks. Being attractive wouldn't solve all my problems like I always thought."

 I eventually introduced Bart to my roommates and he is now one of the best friends I have ever met. I loved his philosophy on life and learned so much from him. When I was younger I used to live by a similar philosophy of realizing how each day is precious and that we really do only get one life on Earth. However, the more and more isolated I became, the less I was able to appreciate each day as a gift. Each day was no longer an opportunity to laugh with people, help people, love, and experience new and exciting things. I was living in a box. I grew more and more comfortable in my box, cut off from the outside world as much as possible. I didn't want anyone to know me because I didn't like me. I began to feel increasingly anxious in conversations. My ability to maintain eye contact was getting worse and worse. The first couple months Bart and I hung out, he helped open my eyes to the world I was missing out on. I had once again become outgoing and was meeting new people. I was freely joking, laughing, and smiling. It was so refreshing to forget about my obsessions for a while.

The dynamic of my friendship with Bart over the next several years was strange though. Even though Bart opened my eyes in so many ways, I was jealous of his appearance. I wanted to look like he did and would still often think about how his life was better than mine because of his appearance. We were at a University of

Miami football game at the Orange Bowl when a girl came up to him and handed over a business card. She said her agency was looking for models. Things didn't end up working out with that agency, but they did with another agency a few years later. Bart became an extremely successful model. He was signed by Ford Model Agency and modeled for huge companies like Saks Fifth Avenue. The fact that he got pursued for modeling at the football game made me envious. That would never happen to me. I would often think how easy it would be to find a quality girlfriend if I looked like him. I had to battle these thoughts while we hung out. I saw so much in his personality, but looking at his exterior was essentially staring face to face with everything that I wasn't yet so badly yearned to be. Throughout our friendship Bart helped bring out a lot of my good qualities. He saw what I was capable of being at my best, while being outgoing and friendly. He saw me introduce my friends to other friends and talk about all the great things I appreciated about everyone in my life. He saw everything I liked about myself. But he also saw me at my worst. He saw me lie in bed when all my friends had to beg me to go out at night to a party or social gathering. When I was so isolated I would make up excuse after excuse to not have to go out in public. My friends tried so hard to break me out of the shell that I would feel so comfortable crawling into. I am forever grateful for that. At the time I just wanted them to go away. I wished they would just accept my excuse for not wanting to go out. Often times I would even believe my own excuse. I would start to believe the reason I didn't want to go out was because I was tired, or didn't have money, or had a big test to study for. Without my friends persistence I would have gotten much more isolated and probably would have become a complete loner.

12

Single

During this time I was approaching my 21st birthday and did some serious reflection. I realized I was staying in a relationship with Laura for the wrong reasons. I still loved her and felt she was an amazing person. But I knew I wanted to travel, live in Florida and hopefully live in California at some point in my 20s while she was set on staying in New Jersey. It was selfish to stay with her. I was only holding onto her out of emotional comfort at that point. I had been too scared to be on my own because I feared all the obsessive appearance thoughts taking over my life completely. I went through a period of brutal honesty where I decided to clean house. I wrote some pressing thoughts in a journal and realized this was something I had to deal with. I flew home in March to end things with her. I spent the entire hour and a half of breaking up explaining how great of a person she was and how thankful I was to have had her in my life. She went home and changed her status on Facebook from "in a relationship" to "single." It was official. I was going to have to stand on my own.

The first month of being single and not needing someone to hold me up was liberating. I definitely missed Laura and knew I still loved her, but the timing wasn't right. It felt good to do something that I knew was right yet left me vulnerable to my insecurities. I travelled on spring break with friends to San Diego and Los Angeles shortly after. I was extremely outgoing during the entire trip. I finally felt like I did in my youth, when I used to start conversations with random people. I used to be loud in class. I didn't care if people were looking at me and certainly didn't care this much about my appearance flaws. At hotels, restaurants, Venice beach- wherever I went, I was asking people for directions, joking around and asking people where they were traveling from.

My mother is the most outgoing person I have ever met. She has made many friends walking my dog, in line at stores, and basically anywhere she has traveled. I loved that I was able to develop this personality trait from watching her throughout my life. Unfortunately it had been buried inside for a long time. This was the first week it really resurfaced in years. I was acting like the person I always wanted to be. I even sent an email to my favorite English teacher in high school and reconnected with him. I didn't have anyone holding me up and didn't feel like I needed to. I was starting to think all my crazy thoughts about my appearance were just part of a phase I went through and I had matured to the point where that silly stuff didn't matter anymore.

One day when we were in Los Angeles I was waiting in line at a supermarket. I picked up a tabloid and saw a zoomed in picture of a celebrity with a big red circle around a mark on her face with the word zit and an arrow pointing to it. I showed it to my friends and laughed about it. I couldn't believe that we lived in a society that deemed a zit newsworthy. In a moment of clarity I was able to understand one of the major contributors to my obsessions with my appearance that started at a young age. At the same time I thought about how fortunate I was to not be a celebrity during my teens. I used to want to be a child actor but would have never been able to handle seeing myself in tabloids. I was thankful for not being famous enough to be in a tabloid and have my appearance scrutinized. After the trip I went back to school and the feelings of freedom and liberation began to wear off a little. The semester ended, I packed up and headed back to New Jersey.

I set off for my thousand mile road trip embarking on a new summer being single. While crossing the Delaware Bridge I started thinking about how none of my friends were going to be home that summer. I started thinking I might be a little lonely. I began contemplating contacting my ex girlfriend. Even though I knew we had different plans for the future, we would both be home for the next few months.

I caved and contacted Laura. She told me not to call her until I moved back to New Jersey for good. I slowly crawled back into my old shell. I got a job at a famous restaurant at the Jersey Shore in Sea Girt called The Parker House for the summer. At orientation I realized there were about twenty other servers working there. And they were all female! This would be most guys' dream. Not for me. Now I would have to worry about my appearance every time I went to work. I was slowly entering a pretty deep depression. All of my close childhood friends were away at school or traveling. All of my Miami friends were back at their homes. I had no girlfriend and no friends for the first time. I enjoyed rainy days at the Jersey Shore that summer. I liked falling deeper into the depression. Sunny days didn't fit in with my gloomy outlook on life.

One night I was serving a single older lady in her late 70s. We got to talking and she told me that all of her siblings married people but she never met a guy that wanted to marry her. She said, "I guess I was just meant to be single." I started thinking about aging. The thought of aging and looking less attractive was terrifying. I would gain weight, get wrinkles, have worse teeth, and all the mirrors would still be there. How did people get older and not become incredibly insecure? I guessed people just cared less about all of those things as they get older. I really hoped that would happen to me. I hoped having a career, a family, experience, and wisdom would help change my thinking. I hoped they would all help me derive less self-worth from my perception of my appearance, because so far getting older had only made things worse.

I wondered if having a wife would make it all go away. Maybe when I got married, I could finally stop beating myself up. If someone actually officially committed to staying with me until death did us part then I could realize I don't have to look attractive for everyone all the time. But I wondered if she would stay with me when I started aging and becoming really ugly. Would she stay with me when she had to look at my increasingly unattractive body and face every single morning and evening for the rest of her life? I spoke to the single older lady a little longer while thoughts about aging ran through my head. I remember going into the bathroom, looking in the mirror and wondering if that was my fate. Was I destined to be alone for eternity?

One night that summer I was watching the HBO television show *Entourage* and wishing I could be a famous actor. I wanted to look like the main character, Vincent Chase, played by Adrian Grenier. It seemed like everyone on TV and in the movies was attractive. I had developed a bad habit over the years when I watched TV shows with a really attractive person. I would stare at the best looking actor for almost the entire episode wishing I could look like him. I would look at each individual feature, yearning to have my deformities replaced with his perfection.

I dreamt of being an actor at one point. When I was younger I thought it was mainly my nose that made me unattractive. After watching shows when I was younger I would look in the mirror and think how I could become famous if I could just fix my nose. But throughout the years I would see advertisements showing something that could be wrong with one's appearance and then offering a cosmetic solution to fix it. Without fail every time I learned one of these imperfections that people can have, I believed I had it. Lips, teeth, nose, head shape, facial shape, skin tone, acne. I struck out on one after another. I was an absolute genetic failure.

With this growing realization, I knew becoming a famous actor was a total fantasy. The thought of having cameras on me actually scared me to death by then anyway. With high definition televisions now available, I realized I had missed my window to be an actor. Maybe before high definition television I would have had a chance. Then my flaws wouldn't have been so glaringly obvious. HDTV would show my horrific skin and every little imperfection in amazing detail.

While fantasizing about becoming an actor during one episode of *Entourage*, I recalled an episode of the cartoon show *The Simpsons*. An older character named Moe wanted to become an actor. There was an accident at his work that somehow altered his appearance and made him become attractive. He had always considered himself ugly before that. His whole life changed when he became good looking and he was able to become an actor. Later on in the episode something happened that reversed the change and he was once again unattractive. After the reversal back to his original appearance, he attended an audition. The casting director said we were looking for someone that is "TV ugly, not ugly ugly." I remember wishing that I was TV ugly that night. I wasn't though. I was so ugly I couldn't even be casted as an unattractive person on TV. I was ugly ugly.

I somehow made it through that miserable summer. I wanted to escape back to Miami several times, but then would remember my friends weren't there either and I would just be all alone down there with the same problems. I was at an all time low.

13

Depression

I got back to school for my senior year and was now 21. I was already on track to take five years to graduate, but this was the 4th and final year for some of my best friends. I was relieved to finally be back around my roommates. I was obsessed with my appearance again. And this time I didn't have a girlfriend to help reassure me that I wouldn't end up alone. I started listening to a lot of music.

In anthropology class, the professor talked about her experience living amongst natives in a jungle. As when Pravin talked about Sri Lanka, I again wished I lived in a culture where appearance didn't seem to matter, one where everyone was only worried about survival. Maslow's Hierarchy of needs explained that human's needs could be defined in a pyramid. At the bottom of the pyramid were physiological needs like food, water, and breathing. Then came areas of security like employment, family, and resources. Then love and belonging with friendship and family. Then self esteem and finally self actualization. I wished that I lived in one of those societies where my worries could be on the bottom of the pyramid. If I was worried about survival I wouldn't have to worry about my looks. If I lived in a primitive society there wouldn't be any mirrors.

This anthropology professor also mentioned a study on the impact the introduction of television in Fiji had on body image and eating disorders of teenage girls. She told us that In the 1990s Dr. Anne Becker and fellow researchers from Harvard Medical School performed a study to examine this impact of the introduction of television in two separate towns of Fiji in the Pacific.

They found that feelings of poor body image and eating disorders were on the rise from the time girls were first exposed to television. Fiji is a country where girls traditionally have healthy and robust appetites and larger body shapes, unlike those portrayed as attractive on television and in magazines. The findings indicated that with exposure to television an alarming percentage of girls began vomiting to control their weight and dieting under the belief that they were overweight and less appealing. Some girls were interviewed stating that they now wanted to look like girls from shows like *Beverly Hills 90210* instead of older women from their culture. (ANNE E. BECKER, 2002)

I thought about the unattainable body image I had been constantly striving for. I thought about wishing I looked like Jonathan Taylor Thomas when I was only 11. I knew images displaying actors and models wearing makeup or using airbrush technologies to hide normal imperfections in billboards, magazines, and pop-up ads weren't real, but it didn't matter. I still wanted to look like the celebrities in those ads. I held myself to that standard of perfection.

Despite becoming increasingly aware of my irrational thoughts, I wasn't able to decrease their prevalence or effect on my mood. This truly was a rough time for me. I was extremely isolated and had been depressed for about four months.

There was one day this Fall when Jim offered to take us out on his boat in Key Largo. Jim's backyard was postcard picture perfect. Throughout college he took me out on his boat a couple times. I loved speeding across the open water and feeling the wind on my face. I loved being surrounded by aqua colored water. As long as I was able to avoid thoughts about my appearance the boat was great. Sometimes we would go with a group of friends and I would feel really self conscious. The wind would mess my hair up and the sun would expose my flaws. I absolutely couldn't take my shirt off and let people see my body. I hated the fact that I couldn't enjoy the experience. I knew we were seeing one of the most beautiful places in the world yet I often couldn't appreciate it. I was too busy thinking about my flaws.

Fortunately on this particular trip to the Keys my thinking was good and we had a wonderful day. It was one of those days where I felt totally in touch with nature and there was a beautiful sunset on the boat ride back to his dock. On the car ride back to Miami I told Jim and Bart that it was one of the best days of my life and that I had been struggling for a long time. I said that I was beginning to wonder if I was ever going to be happy again. I said it was such an amazing feeling to be happy that day. They didn't really have any clue what I was talking about. They probably knew I was acting really distant lately, but didn't understand how deep I was inside of my own head at that point.

A couple of weeks later my roommates planned a trip to Disney World in Orlando. Jim's dad also had an RV which his family used for road trips. He convinced his dad to allow us all to borrow it for a Disney trip during our fall break. I really didn't want to go because I was still feeling very depressed. I was looking forward to spending a few days alone in our house. So, like many times before, my friends were forced to beg me to join them. Jim packed a bag for me while I insisted I wasn't coming. After a couple hours of pleading they finally convinced me. We drove from Miami to Orlando and played video games in the back of the RV on the ride up to the campgrounds. I felt like we were in a band touring the country. The first night there we played miniature golf and one friend looked at a picture he just took and asked why I never showed my teeth while smiling. After making up some weak excuse, all of my friends joined the conversation and told me to start showing my teeth in pictures. I was really self conscious about it now because everyone would be watching for it throughout the trip. I decided to face my fear and smile all weekend. We went to Halloween Horror Nights one night and, while walking in, a girl walked up to me and started flirting. I couldn't believe a random girl started talking to me so I was awkward in the conversation and didn't ask for her number. But the encounter still boosted my confidence for the night. The next day we were walking through the amusement park and during a trip to the bathroom I had a total meltdown. I didn't like the way my hair looked so I soaked it with water and had to use paper towels to dry it. I disappeared for 15 minutes until I had it looking presentable while everyone wondered where I went. I was at Disney World, the most innocent and pure vacation place in America, and all I could care about was my appearance. I couldn't have the fun that Disney offered most visitors. When we got back from the trip, I looked at photos and hated my smile. I removed every picture from Facebook that had my teeth showing. I decided moving forward I would only have pictures of myself that I liked tagged on Facebook. In some silly way, when I looked through all the pictures I liked of myself, I started to believe I always looked like that. It made me feel much better about my appearance when I was tagged in a good picture.

Towards the end of the semester a discussion came up in my English literature course about vanity. I wondered if I was vain. I had heard that word when I was younger in a discussion about beauty only being skin deep. I never really knew what it meant. Vain: excessively proud, especially of personal appearance. OK, that definitely isn't me. Pride in my appearance was nonexistent and I essentially felt worthless because of my looks. To someone on the outside observing my constant mirror checking and conversation about appearance, I'm sure I could have appeared vain. But it couldn't have been further from the truth. I hated the fact that I thought about my appearance so often.

The semester in general was pretty depressing and I was relieved to go back home in the winter. I had four wisdom teeth removed while home during winter break. My swollen cheeks made me look like a chipmunk so I was worried about pictures when a girl we were friends with invited us to a New Year's Eve party. Her father had an office in Times Square in New York City on the street where the ball dropped. A big balcony allowed us to look down 20 floors at the thousands of spectators lined up for the festivities. After arriving and hanging our heads over the balcony looking down the street filled with people, my friend said, "I plan on doing a lot of cool things in life, but I can't imagine many being much cooler than this." We had the best seats in New York City. I had fun, but spent much of the night checking my chubby cheeks in the mirror. I wished I could just enjoy the moment. While there I ran into a kid who went on a date with my ex-girlfriend during the previous summer. Laura had a crush on him growing up and now that we were broken up, she tried dating him. He told me he wasn't interested in her and tried to bond with me over our mutual lack of interest. I pretended to agree with him but felt sick to my stomach when hearing his story. I called Laura after midnight several times and her friend finally answered and said, "Happy New Year, but sorry she doesn't want to talk to you." I had managed to ruin another experience. I hated all of the pictures from that night and within a few weeks de-tagged them all from Facebook.

14

New Obsession- School

I came back to school in the spring and decided to focus on grades as much as I could. I was 21 and figured it was time to buckle down. I also had to look for a way to somehow diminish the negative thoughts. I hadn't been able to fully devote myself to school in a long time because I was always so worried about my relationships and my appearance.

I needed to do something to feel good about myself. School became my new obsession. I took 18 credits and immersed myself in studying. I told everyone that I wanted to get a perfect GPA of 4.0 and wasn't going to let anything get in my way. I spent Friday nights in the library. I wasn't the most efficient studier because much of my time was spent looking in the mirror thinking about my appearance. The library was actually one of the worst places for me to go. I would sit at a computer and have difficulty concentrating. The first floor of our library was a huge open floor with massive ceiling high tinted windows looking out onto the middle of campus. There were circular stations with computers all throughout the open space. The view outside was of a campus lined with exotic looking people and palm trees. When my thinking was good this was an oasis, but that was rare. I had spent hundreds of hours over my years at school looking at the library mirrors. I knew which ones had high traffic and which ones I could hang out at for a long time. I knew about the one upstairs that had bright lighting and how bad I always looked there. I knew that I went up there sometimes because I simply wanted to feel worse. I did this all having to wait for the one or two hours where I could finally concentrate and study effectively. Usually I would just be comparing myself to everyone in the library, attractive girls sitting at the computers, confident guys talking to each other and joking around, couples studying together and flirting. And I would be all alone, unable to study, focusing on everything I didn't have yet wanted so badly.

But at least I didn't have to hang out with friends in uncomfortable social situations. I didn't have to interact with people while studying. The long unproductive library sessions were a great escape from everything. It wasn't healthy but I justified it thinking there were much worse ways I could be spending my time. My friends would ask me to go out and I had the perfect excuse. I told everyone that I hadn't taken school seriously enough in the past and I had to try really hard to make up for it. Part of that was true, but studying mostly served as a way to sink further into isolation. There were some weekend nights where I would be one of the only people in the library. I would start browsing on the internet for surgeries to fix my imperfections. I would then go into the bathroom and look to see if I'd be much more attractive without that flaw. I probably spent less than 25% of my time in the library actually studying.

Getting good grades did make me feel a lot better at times. I was able to obsessively check for grade updates on the course websites and think about getting A's instead of my appearance. A couple times I was mentioned in front of the entire class for my achievements. In a class of 30 people one teacher told everyone I had the highest grade on a particular test. That felt really good. I wasn't accustomed to any kind of recognition. Of course I would have rather been the most attractive person in the class. I convinced myself that getting good grades would fix my problems. My life would be good if I attained good grades. I would get a desirable job and be happy in the future. I was always looking for something to fix my life in the future. I was never happy with how it was at the time.

One night that semester I was standing in the kitchen with my roommates and somehow one of them started talking about how they had a big nose. Then everyone went around in a circle joking about a flaw they didn't like on themselves. When it was my turn I made some comment to change the conversation. I was so scared they would point out a flaw of mine. Which one would they pick? I didn't have the courage to say one myself. If someone mentioned something about one of my flaws existing or even being a tiny bit different than the norm, it was confirmed. I can distinctly remember from a young age every single time someone made mention of my biggest flaws. Not only can I remember when it was said and by whom, I can remember almost exactly what was said and how it made me feel. There was always a slight hope that perhaps it was just in my head. Perhaps it existed but the degree to which others noticed it might be less than what I thought. But once any mention was made of it the result was always the same. CONFIRMATION! I knew it. I knew everyone was looking at it. I knew that's what people noticed when they saw me. They had no idea what they did by saying that. How could they say that to me? Didn't they know they weren't dealing with a typical secure person? One who can handle a comment about a characteristic that is different in any way from societal standards of attractiveness. Sticks and stones may break my bones but words don't hurt at all. Nonsense. I would have rather taken a brutal beating with sticks and stones than hear those agonizing words. Then with my injuries I could justify getting plastic surgery!

At the end of the semester I kind of crashed in school and didn't do great on all my finals. I didn't get the 4.0, but did make dean's list for the first time. I was really disappointed in myself. Once again I had managed to place unreasonable expectations on myself and not live up to them. Throughout the semester I would get so mad if I didn't get an A on any given test. I would obsess about what I had to get on each assignment to get a final grade of an A. This wasn't healthy. I wasn't even enjoying my life. I actually really do enjoy learning new things and putting an effort into my school work. At the time my obsessive approach to school was unhealthy though and I squeezed all of the enjoyment out of learning.

15

Dating

During this school year I had gradually regressed to my stage in high school where I had very little interaction with girls. I once again felt anxiety when talking to anyone of the opposite sex. I no longer could hold down a conversation. One of the worst parts of being insecure was meeting someone new. The possibility of entering into a new relationship was extremely exciting. But it was also filled with a lot of agony. Dating someone would mean all of my fears about feeling unattractive to everyone else could at least be quieted. At least ONE person would find me attractive, or would be able to accept me with all of my flaws. But then the thoughts would come:

What if they were only attracted to me when they first met me because I looked pretty good for myself that day? They didn't really get a good look at me. I read somewhere that people look more attractive at first glance. They couldn't see my whole body. There is no way they will like me when they see my body. They won't still like me if they see me in the morning before showering and fixing myself up. They won't still like me when they see me in unflattering lighting. Should I send a text message or a Facebook message? Maybe I should write on her wall. No then everyone can see that. I should wait until tomorrow. I don't want to come on too strong. I always come on too strong when I like someone. The only people that ever like me are the ones I don't smother, but that's because I am not interested in them. Why is this so hard? I hate having to play this game. If I like her why can't I just text her now?

I've been through this agony many times in my life. I was working at Café Tu Tu Tango again and was about to experience this torture. A girl came up to me and handed me a piece of paper.

 "My friend wanted me to give this to you."

"What is it?"

"It's her phone number. She thinks you're cute"

Me, cute? Was she blind? Well there was dim lighting in the restaurant. Maybe she just didn't get a great look at me. I had longer hair at this point because I was somehow convinced I looked better with long hair. Well I know exactly why I thought that. My senior year of high school I grew it out a little and a couple girls told me they liked my curly hair. I never had been complimented on my hair before. I also thought it hid my unattractive face.

"Really, where is your friend? Why didn't she give it to me?"

"She's over there. She's awesome. She loves to surf and is really adventurous. Don't blow it. She's a great girl."

"OK thanks, I'll call her," I mumbled.

I couldn't believe someone came up to me and gave me her friend's number. I felt so high on life. I went home after work and immediately told all my friends!

"I got a number!" I exclaimed.

I told the story and my roommates encouraged me to call her. I looked her up on Facebook but couldn't find her because I only had her first name. I didn't want to friend her anyway. This was actually the worst part of being single, knowing that I would have to survive the Facebook test with any girl I was interested in. Once we became friends she would inevitably browse through all of my pictures. No matter how bad I looked in person, it was only a memory in someone's mind when we weren't together. The memory of my ugliness might not be so strong. If they saw me on a good day or happened to not be a particularly critical person, they might have even been a little attracted to me. But a picture is right there for everyone to see whenever they choose. And I will eventually get tagged in bad pictures when I'm not near the computer to remove them in time. I had started removing tags regularly. I was jealous of my friends who didn't feel the need to remove them. I couldn't understand how they didn't want to immediately delete unflattering pictures of themselves once they were posted. Didn't they understand that everyone was going to look at that picture and think they were unattractive? Everyone has bad pictures, but when people see them online they assume that is how you look. My thoughts eventually got so bad that I just blocked all of my pictures from everyone. I told friends that I didn't want potential employers to see them and judge me. I also said I hated meeting someone who could feel like they knew everything about me from my pictures. The employer part was a lie. I wasn't even applying for internships or jobs at the time.

I just had to hope the girl who gave me her number wasn't a big Facebook person. I waited a day and texted her.

"Hey, it's Mark, the server from Café Tu Tu Tango. What's up?

"Hi, Mark! How are you? Sorry for my friend. She is so weird."

"I'm great. Happy it's Saturday. It's OK, your friend was funny."

"So I'm going surfing tomorrow. You should come with me. We are going at 9 AM."

Oh great. Now what? I can't go surfing with her. She will see my body at the beach. I look ugly when my hair is wet. She can see all my flaws at the beach. At least if I can date her a few times in other settings she could like my personality and maybe overlook the flaws she will notice later. I need to make up something. I have to say I am doing something that makes me sound good. I can't say I have a test. That will make me look like a nerd, unless she wants a studious guy. I'll just say I made plans with a friend so it looks like I keep commitments.

"Oh that sounds fun but unfortunately I have plans with a friend tomorrow. We should definitely hang out some time though."

"OK. Sounds good."

This girl might be too much pressure. I don't want to have to worry about how I look with her every time we go to the beach. I need to find someone who isn't a big beach person, perhaps someone who only likes hanging out in dimly lit places. Ah who am I my kidding? I need to just date a blind person.

The high from getting her number was wearing off. I spent most of the weekend looking at myself in the mirror, doing my usual routine of picking myself apart and convincing myself I'm never going to find a quality girl that can overlook my flaws. On Monday afternoon she texted me and I had hope again. I was back in excitement mode.

 I would just avoid the scary beach thoughts for now. Nothing else in my life mattered at this point. All of my thoughts were now about her. I knew very little about her, but she was starting to seem perfect for me. Plus she showed interest in me. Everything was riding on this. My entire emotional balance now depended on whether she responded to each text message. I sent a message and started checking my phone, obsessively checking. Two minutes went by. Maybe she was thinking of something to say. Maybe she didn't have her phone on her. My phone started vibrating and read "text received." I thought, "Yes! She liked it. She laughed. I'm witty." We texted back and forth for 20 minutes until she had class. I was never the one to end the conversation. I never said I had to go somewhere. I would miss class to keep talking to her because this was all that mattered now. I was not thinking about my flaws. I was not worried about feeling inadequate. The only thought was the possibility of a new life with her. I felt like I did in 2nd grade when I had a crush on a girl. Butterflies were in my stomach. I should have been studying for a test but couldn't concentrate. She texted me during her class and said her teacher was boring. Yes! She wasn't just blowing me off. We started texting again and I asked her everything about herself. We made great conversation while texting nonstop for four hours. I told her we should hang out the next night and she agreed.

The date was all I thought about for the next 24 hours. I was excited, nervous, and fearful. I made it through the day trying my best to calm my nerves. We met at the parking lot of her college because she went to a different school than me in Miami. She got into my car and I told her we should go to the beach, which was about a 30 minute drive from her campus. I felt her eyes on me the whole ride while we talked. I pulled up to a stop light and the street lights were shining in my car. I wondered how I looked in the lighting. I tried to not think about it. We got to the beach and parked a few blocks away in a parking garage. The Parking garage had bright florescent lights that I usually looked bad in so I couldn't get out of there fast enough. We walked down to the water and sat down in the sand. I loved the beach at night. I didn't have to worry about being the weird guy swimming in a t-shirt at night. The more we talked I realized how uninteresting I had become because the majority of my time was occupied thinking about my appearance. She was motivated and packed a lot into her schedule. I was envious of how much she did with her life. I wanted to be like that, but was so limited now with my obsession about my perceived flaws. Even when I did hobbies I was unable to fully enjoy them. We talked for a couple hours and walked back to the car. We talked some more and listened to music on the car ride home. I dropped her off at her car. We agreed it was a fun night. Driving home I realized the date didn't go that well. All the excitement had deflated. I could tell she wanted a more interesting guy. Maybe if I was better looking she would have given me a chance. I didn't sell her on my personality and that was my only chance. I decided to never text her again. I couldn't handle the emotional swings of the texting. If I sent her a message I would be constantly checking my phone. It was easier to just give up at this point. I figured she would text me if she was interested. She never did and I once again felt hopeless. I was sent further into my shell, into my lonely, isolated world.

16

Dentist

The only reason I hadn't gone into a deep state of depression at that point was that I had great plans for the summer to travel Europe with my college friends. I realized how fortunate I was to meet international students at school. I was still living with Nick, Memo, Jim, and Pravin. We planned to do some traveling on our own before meeting at Memo's house in Istanbul, Turkey. Nick's family had a house in Dusseldorf, Germany, an apartment in Copenhagen, Denmark and a house in Nice in the south of France- all of which we planned to visit. I was the luckiest person on Earth to have met such great guys and be able to travel with them. Unfortunately I didn't know that a good portion of my trip would be spent thinking about my appearance.

I had become increasingly obsessed with my teeth in the months leading up to the trip. During the previous summer when Laura and I officially broke up, I was incredibly self conscious about my smile. I decided I needed to do something about the crooked teeth. I went to the dentist and asked him to shave down my canine teeth because I always hated how sharp they were. I felt great for a few days after he did it, thinking they looked much better and my problems were solved. Within less than a week I became unhappy with my smile again. There was still a space between the canines and my other teeth. My dentist said the only way to fix that would be capping them or getting veneers. During the entire school year, when looking in the mirror or smiling, I constantly thought about fixing my teeth. I was already at the point where I would only smile with my mouth closed. After the Disney trip I knew I needed to do something. I met a friend at college who told me he had a dentist who was a family friend in Alabama and did veneers for a good price. He gave me the dentist's number and let him know I would be reaching out to him. Great! I was going to fix one my flaws. I was worried about all my pictures for the upcoming trip to Europe. I needed to get the procedure done before then. It was a comforting thought every night that spring knowing I was going to fix something that was wrong with my appearance. Every time I looked in the mirror I would think about how I couldn't wait to have a new smile.

I spoke with the dentist and his assistant asked me to email some pictures of my smile. Usually the procedure was done in several visits but I needed to do it all in one session before my trip to Europe. I had no money to pay for this so I decided to take out a loan for the veneers. I was a finance major and knew that taking on debt for a cosmetic surgery was a stupid decision but I didn't care. I would rather have been poor than gone on living with those teeth. Little did I know, it wasn't my external flaws that were my problem. I took tons of pictures for the dentist until I was satisfied that I didn't look too ugly in them. I emailed them over a few days before the semester ended. I had my car packed and was heading to Alabama. I told Pravin and Memo where I was going and they told me there was nothing wrong with my teeth. I figured they were just trying to make me feel better. I drove the 13 hours straight through to Alabama. I looked at my smile every so often in the car and was extremely excited. I was ready to make my first fix to a major flaw. I got to the hotel and could barely sleep. I was terrified that I would miss the appointment and lose my chance.

I arrived at the dentist and we got right to business. It took all day to work on my teeth and fit the veneers. At one point an assistant mentioned how a teenager who was a model recently had his teeth done there. She said he was told he was perfect for modeling except for his teeth which were now fixed. I wondered why she was telling me this story. Why tell this story to an ugly person? I was thinking about how even with my teeth fixed I would still have all my other flaws. No matter how much I fixed, I still had bad skin and a generally unattractive appearance. The permanent flaws were the hardest ones to think about. I couldn't even dream of fixing them. I received several painful shots of a local anesthetic. He shaved down my teeth and fitted the veneers. He meticulously placed each veneer and spent hours working like an artist. We finished one of the more unpleasant days of my life and I walked out and checked out my new teeth in the car mirror.

It happened to be my 22nd birthday and I was spending it all alone. I called my mom on the way back to the hotel and told her the teeth were done. I wasn't sure if I liked them and started freaking out. I just did an irreversible procedure and thought I might not like it. I was still really swollen so I wouldn't be able to assess the final result for a few days. I was wondering if people would notice the change and how much I would be judged if they did. I figured my teeth were the most socially acceptable flaw I could fix. If I got a nose job people would undoubtedly judge me.

I stopped in Maryland and stayed with a good friend of mine named Anna. I became very good friends with Anna during my time at school in Miami. We knew a lot about each other and both had a great respect for one another. I knew she wouldn't judge me for having my teeth fixed. I drove up to her house and was incredibly anxious to see her reaction. She told me the new teeth looked great and made me feel much better about the procedure. I drove to New Jersey the next day to prepare for my journey to Europe. Although pleased with the outcome, the procedure didn't solve my problems. I was still unhappy with so many things about my appearance. It wasn't my appearance that needed to be fixed. I needed a complete mental makeover.

17

Europe

On the trip to Europe I started off solo in Granada, a small city in southern Spain. I studied there for three weeks. The first week I stayed with a Madre and had no roommates. I barely spoke Spanish and she had a heavy accent and spoke in the Andalucian dialect. I was used to hearing Castillano which was taught in American schools and spoken in Madrid.

The first night I put my headphones on and walked up to the Alhambra Castle alone. As I walked through the city and on the trail up to the castle I noticed every person in Spain had a great tan. Their skin was so much better than mine. There were more attractive people than me everywhere I went. The garbage men looked like models. Hippies sitting on the street playing guitar looked so much more confident than me. It looked like they hadn't showered in days. I got on the path going up to the castle and turned up the music to quiet my thoughts. When I got to the top my jaw dropped. The views were breathtaking. I stood there and looked over the whole city of Granada. The old lit up houses alongside the mountain were beautiful. I was happy I decided to take this trip to Europe and excited for the summer. I liked being alone more and more. I wanted to take these next few weeks as a time to grow before meeting up with my friends. I never did anything like this before. I usually needed to be around other people I knew at some point during the day to break up the insanity of my thoughts. I walked back down the hill, went into a restaurant and asked to use their bathroom. The mirrors wrapped around the whole bathroom. They met at the corner of the walls and I looked at myself so half my face was on the mirror to the left and the other half was on the mirror to the right. Somehow I had never really done this before. I noticed how much I lacked symmetry in my face.

I recalled reading earlier that spring how models are mostly symmetrical. Features on models faces are even on both sides, another qualification that I couldn't meet. I read this in my school library. We had a section of our library called "the stacks" at the University of Miami. It was eight or nine floors of books with desks along the walls and windows overlooking the campus and surrounding city. There were bars on the windows. It was basically a prison with excellent views. I would go up there to get away from everyone. I picked up a random old psychology book that spring and saw a section on which features were generally considered attractive for men. Neat hair, symmetrical face, small nose, fit body. I remember thinking how stupid it was to try to generally explain attractiveness like this. I also remember striking out on all of these characteristics, from my perception anyways.

I analyzed my asymmetrical face some more and then walked home excited for the first day of class. During

Spanish class the next day my teacher mentioned Brad Pitt and I said I wish I looked like him. She said, "You must do OK with the ladies with your blond curly hair." I just giggled. I could never take anything that resembled a compliment, always assuming people were only trying to make me feel better.

I would go to a local supermercado every day where one woman named Maria working at the register was stunningly gorgeous. I would go to Maria's line every day and try to think of something funny to say. I never was able to say anything. I figured she probably didn't speak much English anyways and my Spanish wasn't great. That was my excuse to not try and talk to her.

One night I was hanging out with a kid I met in class. We went to some kind of carnival and on the way home he started talking to me about girls. Somehow the conversation got to the point where he was talking about a counselor he saw. He said that something the counselor told him really made sense. She said if someone of the opposite sex doesn't give you a chance without getting to know you, their actions are out of your control and can't be taken personally. She told him that he should strive to have people want to associate with him based on his personality and attributes that aren't visible with the eye. I wondered why he was telling me this. He must have sensed that I was insecure and struggling like he was. Maybe he told me because he thought I was ugly. That was probably it.

One night in Spain a few of us students from the school went out to a cafe. Two girls I talked to from Austria were beautiful. At the end of the night I said to one girl who had gorgeous blue eyes, "You have awesome eyes. I love them." In an Austrian accent she said, "Thanks. I like your teeth." This made me laugh. I wasn't sure whether to take it as a compliment or be embarrassed that my new bright white teeth were so noticeable. One of the girls asked me who my favorite soccer player was. I didn't know many players but had recently wished I looked like Cristiano Ronaldo from Portugal. Memo had a soccer magazine with him on the cover in our bathroom back in Miami. Every time I went to the bathroom and saw his face I wished I had his skin and hair. I said he was my favorite player and the Austrian girl laughed. She told me that her guy friends would make fun of me if they heard I liked that "pretty boy."

My key to the apartment building didn't always work and I would have to sit on the stoop until someone else entered the apartment. I would sit down and watch beautiful and happy Spanish people walk by in groups. I felt very lonely. I couldn't take living alone anymore with the Madre that I barely understood so after my first week in Spain I requested an apartment change. I was falling into a mild depression and started sleeping in instead of going to my Spanish classes. They weren't for credit, but I was still wasting money and an opportunity to learn. The program's housing coordinator put me in an apartment where another lady was hosting eight students. Several girls currently staying in the apartment were Mormons from Utah. I became friends with them quickly and we had a lot of fun together. They didn't make me nervous like most girls did at the time. They told me they were going on a trip to Morocco with a big group of people from Utah and I decided to join along. We drove on a bus down to the south of Spain and then along the coast and took a ferry across the Strait of Gibraltar. We were taking pictures on the ferry and I was trying to tame my hair in the wind. I was thinking how great it would be to look good with short hair and not have to worry about my hair all the time. I stayed in a hotel room with the Mormon girls in Morocco. In the morning I showered and changed in the bathroom and then hung out with the girls while they all got ready for the day. I had to let my hair air dry to look the way I wanted it but hated the way I looked with wet hair. They were all going to see me at my worst. I hated that feeling. When I really felt like I didn't look good, I couldn't make eye contact with anyone. They saw me in the morning and it wasn't as bad as expected. I was able to endure it, but now they all knew how ugly I was capable of looking.

We were on the bus driving to one of the tourist stops in Morocco and one girl said, "You know I don't normally look like this. When I have makeup on and everything I am really pretty. I look a lot different." I wondered why she said that. She said it kind of out of nowhere. I thought that she probably had some of the thoughts that I have. I wished I could say to everyone I saw when I looked bad for myself," I swear I am usually not *this* ugly."

Another girl mentioned that her family would joke about how she had a melon shaped head. I wondered how in the world she could say that out loud. Didn't she know that everyone would be inspecting her head now? My sister is an occupational therapist and used to work at a hospital with children. She said when kids would complain about their appearance or anything they didn't have, the therapists would say, "You get what you get and you don't get upset." It was a simple little saying that I wished I could live by. I wondered why I couldn't be like the girl who thinks she has a melon shaped head. She didn't seem phased by it. She must have learned to accept herself for how she looked.

After studying in southern Spain without anyone I knew for three weeks, I was ready to venture up to Barcelona to meet Jim. He explored Barcelona for a few weeks and studied there while I was in Granada. I went to the train station with my packed bags but realized I had read the time wrong on my ticket and subsequently missed the train. My best option was to take a bus the next morning out of Granada to Madrid and then switch to another bus. I was stuck with my luggage and walking around the city alone. I ran into a group of Italians who were living in the city. They sensed my frustration and after some small talk invited me to hang out with them for the night. I ended up going out dancing with them at a 'discoteca' even though I felt really self conscious dancing. I figured if I made a fool of myself I would never see these people again. One girl lived next to the train and offered to let me crash at her place until the morning. She was just being nice and wasn't interested in me or anything like that. She let me sleep on her couch. When I took the bus the next morning I wondered if she had liked me and I had been too shy to try and kiss her. I thought about how ugly I was and settled on the thought that she was just an exceptionally nice person. I was glad I didn't try to kiss her and put her in an uncomfortable position.

After a day long journey I arrived in Barcelona. I had Jim's address and it was somewhere on a street called Aribau. We didn't really have reliable cell phones on the trip so I was hoping Jim would be there. Unfortunately he was already out at a festival at the beach. I wondered how the heck people used to coordinate anything before cell phones. I called him a few times and finally got through to him with the help of one of his roommates. I went down to the festival at the beach and we walked around the crowds of thousands of people. I hated being in big crowds. Besides staring at every attractive person and wishing I looked like them, I felt so insignificant. A couple of women from China asked to take a picture with me. They were pointing at my curly hair which was bleached blonde and I guess it was rare for them to see. I thought how they would realize how unattractive I was when they saw me in the picture later on.

 We met up with more friends from college and traveled to Prague, Istanbul, several cities in Italy, Paris, Amsterdam, Copenhagen, Germany, and Nice. It could have been the best two months of my life had I not been constantly thinking about my appearance. I had a wonderful opportunity to meet people from all over the world, but was too insecure to talk to anyone. We rented a boat in Capri, Italy and a local told us that George Clooney visited there often. During the entire day on the boat I wished that I looked like George Clooney. I absolutely hated the way I looked in pictures that day. I was pale and greased up from sun block. I would go back and forth from enjoying the beauty of Capri to hating the fact that I was personally lacking any beauty. We swam in the Blue Grado, the most amazing natural sight my eyes have ever seen. I was able to enjoy it briefly.

When the trip was over I reflected in a notebook about all of the different places we stayed. I slept in over 20 different beds throughout the two months and saw so much. I started looking through pictures and couldn't help but think about the way I looked instead of appreciating each memory. I didn't look at the scenery or anyone else. I repeated my habit of staring at myself and analyzing how I looked in each picture. I remembered whether or not I was happy at the time the picture was taken based on how I felt about my appearance at that moment. If I liked my hair, I remembered being happier.

I got back home and went on my annual family vacation to Maine. My family has rented a cabin on a lake in Maine nearly every year since I was six years old. Maine is my sanctuary. The place we visit never changes. Even the docked boats in the water seem to be in the same exact location every year despite being removed every winter. We take pictures there from year to year and I swear everything looks identical. One of the great things about Maine is the bathroom mirror in the house that we stay in. It is pretty much the only mirror I look in during the entire trip. Somehow the lighting in that bathroom makes me look more tan than usual and hides a lot of my blemishes. I've always loved the way I look in it. If I looked that way in real life I would be a happy man.

Happy Gilmore is a silly Adam Sandler movie I watched growing up that mentioned thinking about your "happy place" to block out all distractions. The lake my family and I go to in Maine is my happy place. It's just me and my family. I don't have to look good for anyone. The sun sparkles off the water and the feeling of sitting on our dock simply can't get any better. It was especially nice being with my family that summer after being in such foreign places in Europe for the previous two months.

18

Final year of college

After Maine, I headed back to Miami for my fifth and final year of college. This time I was determined to change things. I needed to fix my thinking and my life. I was again focused on grades. I always wanted to get involved on campus so I joined the Ethics Debate team. The debate team at my school beat West Point to become national champions the year before. I was trained by some of the smartest people I ever met. I was extremely focused on school but still was a complete wreck emotionally with no balance in my life. I had always dreamed of meeting my future wife at the University of Miami. It was such a great school and I figured we would at least both have a common love for warm weather and our incredible school. My chances were dwindling and I really didn't go out much that semester. I became very isolated from my roommates. My big final debate on campus made me nervous and I stayed up most of the night practicing. When I came home exhausted the next day, my new roommate Terry had friends over for a BBQ after his lacrosse practice. I had started judging people for partying and didn't like that I was becoming this way. Terry left my ketchup bottle out in the sun for two days after the party before I noticed it. I ended up getting in an argument with him about it. He told me that ketchup isn't refrigerated at restaurants, but I insisted that it was ruined because it was in a plastic bottle baking in the sun. I realized I was having a harder and harder time dealing with people. Even my best friends were annoying me over silly things. I was so far from that person I wanted to be when I wrote my college entrance essay. I didn't know how to deal with reality. I just wanted to be a normal person so badly, but was incapable of it. The only way I knew how to get a handle on my obsession with my appearance was to replace it with another obsession-which in this case was school and academic clubs.

I met a girl who was a lifeguard on campus at our Wellness Center. She looked exactly like my ex-girlfriend, Laura. Jim noticed how much she looked like Laura and told me it was weird that I was interested in dating a girl that essentially looked like her twin. I talked to her at the pool a couple times and asked her on a date. We ended up hanging out on campus and getting lunch together. When we were walking around the cafeteria I saw her look in a mirror and fix her hair up. I thought this was a good sign because she wanted to look good for me. I also hoped she was a little insecure which would make me feel less pressure to look good. I decided to smile often and show her that I was a happy person which I hoped would hide my growing depression. I probably smiled for the entire time we ate lunch and she must have thought something was wrong with me. She told me how passionate she was about the ocean and that her major was marine biology. She saw I didn't have many hobbies and probably thought I wasn't very interesting. I texted her the next night and she never responded. I was losing hope.

I had officially reached the point where I didn't even care if I felt attractive anymore. I just wanted to stop thinking about my appearance. I was jealous of people who didn't fit the traditional standards of attractiveness yet seemed happy and unconcerned with their looks. I felt eyes on me all the time when I was in public. I made every attempt possible to engage in eye contact with the opposite sex as a pedestrian on campus, in town, at events- wherever I walked. If I made eye contact and we stayed engaged I felt good. If she quickly looked away I felt repulsive. Maybe she just didn't like eye contact with strangers, I rationalized. Then I thought, "Who am I kidding? I am ugly." I tried to give myself the benefit of the doubt, but my constant uncontrollable self-deprecation was too powerful. At parties and social settings I tried to make eye contact with girls to gauge interest. They would always look at my friends instead of me. I couldn't compete with my friends. Not only were they better looking than me, they didn't care how they looked. Their lack of obsession with their appearance translated into confidence that I could only dream of. As good as I was at attempting and occasionally making awkwardly long eye contact with strangers through that odd game of self torture I played, I couldn't hold eye contact in a real conversation for the life of me. I would constantly look at the ground while talking to people. I didn't know what to say. I was too distracted by the fact that I was probably being analyzed feature by feature. When I did stare at people in conversations, I was looking at their physical characteristics to compare them to my own. "Her body isn't that great either. I wonder if she thinks about it all the time like I do. What perfect skin he has. I would kill for that skin. I bet he doesn't even appreciate it." I don't know what was worse: when someone didn't have any noticeable flaws or when someone had many flaws and just didn't seem to care about them. After coming to the conclusion that I was nearing a breaking point, I headed home to see my family that winter after finals.

I was at my sister's apartment in New York City a few days after Christmas and looking through her digital camera at pictures from the past week. I saw one that really made me look unflattering and had to erase it. I pulled the picture up and deleted it. The only problem was I accidentally deleted every picture from the entire week. My heart sank. I didn't tell anyone why it really happened. We were able to download software that recovered some of the pictures. After this event I knew I needed help. I couldn't live my life like this. The fear of an unflattering picture making its way to Facebook was so powerful. Deleting all the pictures from my family's Christmas week was a sign. Something had to drastically change within me.

19

Counseling

I got back to campus for my final semester and knew I had to get professional help, so I went to the counseling center on campus. I waited in the lobby to see someone and my mind started racing.

I am in a world all alone, almost 7 billion people and counting. That is 7,000,000,000 humans with nine zeros. And here I am completely alone. Nobody understands what I am going through. Maybe there are some other people out there who are upset with their appearance, but nobody can be as bad as I am. I wish I could talk to people about it without appearing vain. The embarrassment is too much. They might commit me to a psych ward. Maybe I am crazy on some level. I can't be insane, can I? It was never like this. It wasn't this bad when I was younger. I was able to go to school and hang out with friends and play sports without these dominating thoughts. I don't know at what point I crossed the line, but I am here. I am at the point where I can't go more than five minutes without thinking about the way I look. If I found someone else that was going through this it would be so much easier. If somehow I was able to admit to another struggling person how I feel, then we could talk about our obsessions and maybe I wouldn't feel so crazy. What is taking them so long? Alright, I need to be completely honest when I get called in. I am just going to spill it all out because my life has become unmanageable. There is no benefit to keeping this in anymore.

"Mark, he's ready for you, third door on the right."

I did an initial intake session with a man and he set me up with a counselor to see. I had problems and I wanted them to go away. I could hardly wait for the next session. A couple days later I met with a woman named Stacy.

"Hi, Mark. My name is Stacy. I will be your counselor. I was reading over your file and there isn't too much in there. I understand you are having some issues with your appearance."

"Yea, Stacy. First things first. I don't mean to sound paranoid, but I see you have a notepad there. Who will have access to these notes?"

"Oh, these are just for me. And my supervisor can read them. But nobody outside of here will be able to read these. There are strict confidentiality laws regarding this."

I was so nervous about anyone ever being able to see how screwed up my thinking was. I was letting her know out of desperation. Life was becoming unlivable. However, I could not leave open even the slightest possibility that anyone else could learn about the insanity that goes on in my head. It would be mortifying. And maybe certain people didn't notice some of my flaws. I couldn't introduce people to the flaws they hadn't noticed yet.

"So what is it that you are having trouble with?"

"I am constantly thinking about my appearance. I don't like the way I look. There are several things I don't like. I don't have any self confidence and I just want to stop obsessing over my looks."

"What specifically do you dislike?"

"Well mostly my overall general appearance. I never liked my body shape and I have bad skin and some scarring from acne."

I wanted to spend the entire hour talking about specific characteristics I didn't like. I wanted to tell her I have always hated my nose. I wanted to tell her I didn't like pretty much every individual feature in addition to my body size and shape. But I didn't want to seem crazy. I would have left there and analyzed and reanalyzed each reaction she had as I mentioned each feature I hated. I would have studied each reaction for validation. That was too terrifying. I feared that she would tacitly agree with my idea that plastic surgery could fix my nose and skin. Some issues couldn't be fixed by plastic surgery. I felt that saying them out loud would somehow make their existence more real. Speaking about them would cement their inescapably permanent existence on my body.

"I spend a lot of time looking in the mirror. Sometimes I go to make sure my hair is in place and there's no food in my teeth. And before I know it I have been in the bathroom for half an hour picking myself apart."

"How do you feel when you are looking at yourself? Run me through a bathroom experience as best you can."

"I feel bad. I really feel sorry for myself. It hurts to think about normal looking people. When it gets really bad I feel like life isn't worth living if I look the way I do. Sometimes I feel like I don't even want to leave the house. It starts out somewhat harmless. I fix my hair. Part it to the side so it looks right. Then I start looking at my nose. I notice my skin looks bad in the light. I look at my body. I try hard to look at myself in more flattering angles- but that doesn't last long. I quickly go back to unflattering angles."

"OK I see. If you can- and I understand it's not easy- but try and go through actual thoughts. Try and put your thoughts in front of the mirror into words. Take your time"

"Well when I look at my nose I might say, 'Why do I have this nose? Why couldn't I have gotten my father's nose? Even my brother and sister have similar ones, but they don't look like this. Almost everyone in class today had a normal nose. God I hate my skin. It's totally unevenly toned. Everyone else gets a nice even tan. I am so pale. How could anyone ever be attracted to this body? No matter how hard I try with diets and working out, my body always looks terrible with my shirt off because of my skin.' These self deprecating sessions often go on for a long time."

"OK. I think we can definitely help you. I work with some people, mostly girls at this point, who struggle with body image and I am confident we can do some good work together. We have a couple kinds of treatment options that we can go with. Typically we do a couple sessions and then reassess if more treatment is desired. We can see each other every other week or weekly. What do you think?"

"How about daily?" She laughed. "No, I'm kidding. I would definitely like to see you weekly if that's possible. And I don't think this is going to be an easy fix, I'm sorry to say."

"I do happen to have a slot open for a semester long treatment. I don't know if you want to commit to that. But I can book you now for the remainder of the semester."

"Perfect. That sounds great."

"Also, we have a group of people that are struggling with body image that meet together weekly and you might want to consider that at some point if you feel comfortable."

"OK. We'll see. I'm not ready for that at this point."

There was no way I could imagine going to a group like that on campus. That sounded terrifying. I left and felt a kind of high again from talking about my issues. I couldn't believe I just told someone a lot of my most embarrassing thoughts. I had all of that bottled up for years. I couldn't believe I just opened up like that to a total stranger. It felt good. I was still trying to make eye contact with every girl I walked by, but I felt better.

I had been single for almost two years at this point. Being single was tough. I would constantly think about being alone. I would wonder if I'd ever find someone that could look past my flaws. I remembered my thoughts being much better when I was in a relationship, even though they really weren't. I would look at girls on campus and think about approaching them but rarely did. When I finally was able to talk to them, I would be so nervous that I couldn't be myself. Not that I really knew what 'myself' even was at this point.

After a few counseling sessions, I met a German girl named Sabrina, who was an exchange student for a year, in a class of mine. I was feeling a little more confident. I somehow mustered the courage to start a conversation with her. Sabrina was pretty receptive so I decided to send her a message on Facebook and we started talking. It was very exciting. My hair had been long for years at this point because I was still convinced I looked better that way. Around that time my friend Anna said that the only reason a guy should have long hair is if he hates his face and feels the need to hide it. I thought, "That's me!" I actually was really tired of having to maintain long hair. With Anna's encouragement and a little confidence from the counseling, I finally decided to cut it. I was so terrified because the barber cut it much shorter than I had asked. I would have never been able to ask for a cut that short because I did believe it would expose my unattractive face. I didn't tell my counselor, Stacy, that the really short cut was partially a mistake when she commended me for how much I took off. Sabrina later admitted I wasn't her type when I had long hair and she probably wouldn't have given me a chance if I had approached her last semester.

My thoughts about my appearance dominated the time that Sabrina and I dated. I constantly wondered why she was willing to date me. A couple months into the relationship she said something about my nose when we were at the Botanical Gardens on a date. She joked that it looked like one of the stuffed animals in the gift shop. She probably thought it was a harmless joke. Up until that point I had thought that she somehow never noticed my funny nose. I thought maybe she was just oblivious. We had a really personal conversation about appearance around that time and Sabrina mentioned many things she used to be insecure about as a teenager. I was able to relate to everything she said. I wondered if she was still insecure about all of those characteristics and simply didn't want to admit it. I thought how it took so much courage to point out her once perceived imperfections to me. Wasn't she worried that I would stare at them from now on, or even worse, break up with her if I hadn't previously noticed them? She spoke as if her feelings of insecurity were part of a phase that she grew out of. I again hoped that my obsessions were also part of a phase like this. Shortly after this, I had a session with Stacy about my fears.

"Mark, I want to talk about your fears today. I was thinking a lot about our last few sessions and I think it's important for you to explore your fears."

"What do you mean, like sharks and snakes?"She laughed.

"No. I mean in relation to your concerns about your appearance. You struggle with a lot of aspects of your appearance. What scares you about not being as attractive as you want to be?"

"Well, I think people judge me based on my appearance."

"Do you think the people that love you have ever treated you differently because of your appearance? Do you think your siblings, parents, or best friends ever treated you differently because of how you look?"

"Well, no. That would be silly. They like me for me. I guess my fear is girls then. I am worried I won't attract a girl."

"But you did have a girlfriend in the past who you were attracted to. You have another one right now who you like. You are obviously able to attract a partner."

"I know, but I think I tricked them. Or maybe they don't care that much about appearance. I don't know. And I'm always scared the girl I'm with will find someone better than me."

"So is it fair to say that the fear at the root of all of your concerns is being alone?"

"I suppose. I don't know why I want to look good all the time. I even want to look good in front of my family and male friends, people that are not sexual to me. But if I am really honest, it's the fear of being alone that scares me the most, or the fear of having to settle for a partner that I am not physically or emotionally attracted to."

This was a deep session with Stacy. I thought a lot about my work in counseling and realized I had been making some serious progress with the sessions. I decided it was time to open up to my good friend Anna. She deserved to know why I had acted so strange and distant many times throughout our friendship. She knew about my veneers but I did a good job of convincing her that was my only major issue with my looks. It was a big step but I was ready to tell a friend about my struggles. I felt comfortable telling Anna. I asked her if she wanted to grab lunch in the cafeteria. Throughout college, we had spent countless hours hanging out in the cafeteria after finishing meals, talking about life, our dreams and everything in between. I never once told her about my obsession with my appearance. I wanted her to think I was a confident guy because she had that impression of me when we met her freshman year. During the first week of classes, new students walk down fraternity row and stop by all of the houses. Four years ago Anna had walked up to the Pike house with some friends and I was feeling confident because I had just moved in and hadn't become isolated yet. I joked around with her and we instantly became friends. She had this positive first impression of me and I was able to maintain it throughout the years of our friendship. There were certain friends I felt more confident around in public. I can't explain why, but certain people made me feel less anxiety and I felt more able to be myself in their company. Anna was one of them. We walked around the buffet stations and brought our trays back to the table. I figured I would get right into it. I had already told her that I wanted to talk.

"So Anna, I'm sure you have noticed that I've acted pretty distant at times the past few years."

"Well yea, that's an understatement."

"I know. I know. I wanted to explain a little bit of my behavior."

"OK."

"Well, it's not easy to tell you all of this. I haven't really ever talked about this with any friends or anyone else in my life."

"Is everything alright?"

"Oh yea yea. Well sort of. I've been seeing a counselor on campus. I have some serious issues. They're all in my head though."

"What do you mean?"

"Well, I've always hated the way I look. I just never felt that attractive. It isn't one thing in particular, I just never felt attractive overall."

I couldn't tell her each feature I didn't like. I had only started telling the counselor some of the individual features I hated, and I just wasn't ready for that.

"Really? You always seemed confident around me. That's kind of surprising."

"Yea, I tried hard to act confident, but I'm not. I just bought into the whole media thing I think. I always wanted to be attractive like people on TV since I was a kid. You're a psychology major. You know how random studies always say that attractive people get treated better throughout life. I think my mind is particularly vulnerable to all of this."

"Yea, but that's silly. Those are superficial benefits. People who get those benefits from being really attractive aren't getting really meaningful relationships or anything. They are just getting shallow people to talk to them or be friends with them. You have real friends. You have such quality friends in your life."

"I know. I understand. It's so much more than that. I can't explain it."

"No, I understand. I knew someone that had bad acne scars on their face and always hated them. It is tough being at our college with so many attractive people, too."

"Yes, exactly! Well that certainly doesn't make things easier. But the truth is, it's all in my head. Conceptually, I know that I shouldn't care so much about my appearance. I just can't help it. It affects my mood so much sometimes and that's really why I wanted to tell you about this. So many times throughout college I just wanted to be alone because of these thoughts."

"I see. Well that does explain a lot. Mark, I appreciate you being honest with me. This isn't easy to talk about."

She could see I was starting to become a little less comfortable talking about it. I wasn't making eye contact anymore.

"Thanks. I'm glad you aren't judging me."

"Why would I judge you, Mark? Everyone has problems. I know so many people who see counselors for problems. "

"I know. I just feel stupid, because this is all in my head. It's not like I experienced a tragic event that I can't get past. I feel like I brought this problem on myself and I should be able to just stop thinking this way."

"Don't feel stupid. I get what you're saying, but it's not that easy. If people were able to stop thinking a certain way that easily, psychologists and psychiatrists wouldn't have much work. I'm just proud of you for getting help to deal with it."

"Thanks. It's definitely helping. Some days are better than others, but I definitely feel an improvement. I know we always talk about being grateful for things. I try to focus on a few things that I am grateful for each day and that's been helping some."

"OK, good. And I just want to let you know, if you ever are struggling with anything you can always talk to me about it. I'm always here for you."

Wow! What a relief. I wasn't sure what to expect. I thought she was going to look at me like I had two heads. Well I guess I knew deep down she would probably be understanding. Otherwise I wouldn't have felt comfortable telling her. Things were never awkward when we hung out after that. I was a little worried that I might feel extra self conscious in front of her in the future, but never did. Telling someone was almost like taking a weight off my shoulders. Telling a counselor was one thing, but telling a friend was completely different. I've had friends tell me they didn't like one particular feature before, like their hair, nose or weight. But to tell someone that I generally feel ugly and often obsess over it was another story.

20

Tampa and the Barber

My final semester at Miami came to an end and I said goodbye to Stacy. I told her that she would probably never be able to fully grasp the impact our sessions had on my life. Despite the assurance of confidentiality, speaking to another human being about my obsessions was the most terrifying thing I had ever done.

Jim and I sat together during our graduation ceremony and I thought about many of my memories from college during the two hours. We took pictures outside while sweating in our black gowns in the Miami heat. Sabrina met my family for the first time. My parents rented a house down in Key Largo next to Jim's family and my brother and sister stayed with us for the week. My parents knew I was thinking about trying a long distance relationship with Sabrina. My father pulled me aside and told me it was unrealistic to think a pretty girl like her wouldn't meet another guy in Germany. It was rare for him to offer any advice about personal affairs. I didn't want to hear it.

I spent every minute of Sabrina's last week in Miami with her in denial that our lives were about to change. I was terrified of being alone again. It had been two years, and I finally found a girl that could tolerate my ugliness. She wrote me a card on my 23rd birthday before her departure that made me feel like she would be fine if we didn't end up staying together. She had mentioned a few times possibly going to graduate school in America if we stayed together. This made me so happy but she now was entertaining the possibility of her departure being the last time we would see each other. Despite my progress with counseling, my happiness was still almost entirely tied to our relationship. I took her to the airport and kissed her goodbye. I watched her walk through customs and we waved goodbye while she looked back a few times. It was like a scene out of a movie. We had one final wave and when I got back to my car I looked at myself in the mirror before pulling away. I knew I was going to have to stand alone again. I had to figure out if my progress was only because I had a girlfriend. She flew back to Europe and I was scared to be alone. We continued to talk on Skype every day. I sometimes talked to her for 5 or 6 hours at a time- or even longer! Jim moved back to Key Largo with his family and Terry, who had replaced Pravin for our 3rd year in the off campus house, moved back to Long Island, NY. I had a really nice apartment lined up in Downtown Miami with Nick and Memo starting in August, but was going to be all alone for the final months of our lease in the old house. I had so many memories in that house and it was tough to leave. The housing market had crashed in the country and Miami was at the epicenter of it all with uninhabited luxury buildings. We got really cheap rent in a luxury apartment starting in August, but I didn't have a job lined up yet. I found a sales position on the west coast in Tampa. I figured I would give the job a shot but continue to apply to jobs in Miami in the meantime.

After arriving in Tampa, I realized I was not equipped to meet people on my own. All the years of negative thinking and isolation had changed me to an introvert. I quickly learned to hate my job and my life. Eating became my new hobby. It was easy for me to go out and eat until my heart was content when feeling down. The eating got worse as I got deeper into a lonely depression. When things were really bad I would frequent pizza and sushi buffets alone. Living in Tampa with no friends made food an easy choice for dealing with my loneliness. Tampa made me realize how close I was to my friends in Miami and how long it took to build the bonds we had forged. I started obsessing about flying to Germany to visit Sabrina. I made one big sale and booked a two week trip to Munich. I waited for the paycheck to arrive to get the heck out of Tampa. I sent Memo and Nick a Facebook message and told them things didn't work out in Tampa and I would still be moving in with them in August. While I was waiting for payday I decided to get a haircut.

****

A trip to the barber

There are a handful of situations I encounter where my issues with my appearance are quite transparent and inescapable. The beach without a shirt on is an obvious one. People seeing me in the morning before fixing myself up is another. But getting a haircut happens to be one of the worst. I know exactly how I want my haircut. It is such a delicate process to minimize my ugliness. Sometimes if done right I can even look attractive- at least from certain angles. I go in there and sit down and the stylist asks, "How would you like it today?" I always mumble something. I am never able to give my long list of instructions. I think people in the hair salon will think I'm crazy. The stylist will think I'm nuts. I say what I think is most important and always end with, "Not too short!" And then I just pray. Each snip of the scissors is painful. I'm managing a mix of positive anticipation and terrifying fear regarding the final product. Part of me believes that I will look like a totally different person and this haircut could change everything. I am thinking, "If this woman only knew how much is on the line- my happiness or severe depression over the next few weeks." All this is going through my head while I am forced to look at my face straight on in the mirror. The stylist is constantly jerking my head around because I am staring at myself. It's painful for me to look at myself for extended periods of time from this angle. When I'm alone in the bathroom I am in control. I can look at myself at a bad angle for a certain period of time, beat myself up, but then look away when it gets too uncomfortable. I can look at myself from a more favorable angle for a little. I can change the lighting to make my defects less noticeable. Not while getting a haircut. It is a painfully long experience of looking straight ahead. She finishes up and asks how it looks. I never know. I always hate how they style it. Even if it's a good haircut, I will have to style it my own way. I get up from the chair and check the mirrors as I walk up to the register. I hope it's not a total screw up. I am usually just not sure until I get home and wash it once. Once in a while I feel great about it. A great haircut elevates my mood to a completely abnormal level of happiness. You might be thinking it's just a haircut, right? Not for me. There's so much more at stake. Whether or not I can feel comfortable going out into public is at stake.

I walk to my car and check myself in every store window and car window I can see without being noticed too much. I get into my car and check the mirror for a minute. I look around the parking lot to make sure nobody catches me. I can't have a random stranger knowing about my obsession. As I am driving home I look at the mirror at every stop light. I am driving looking back and forth from the road to the mirror. I almost hit a car in front of me. I think, "Wow I need to get this problem under control." I get home and go into the bathroom and shower or wet my hair and then style it my own way.

The next few days I have a feeling of excitement and nervousness every time I check a mirror if it's a relatively good haircut. If it's a bad haircut I am depressed and thinking about exactly how long it will take to look normal again. It seems like an eternity. On multiple occasions I have returned shortly after the haircut and asked them to fix it. Other times I have gone to another place to have it fixed. One time in Miami I said, "Sorry for being so difficult, my head is kind of a funny..." I paused and she said, "Shape," while nodding her head in agreement. I couldn't believe she just agreed with me. How could she do that? Once again, confirmation. I don't even want to go out and see my friends if it's really bad. At least I can wear a hat. But what if someone notices that my hair looks shorter and asks to see? Not only will I have to show them a bad haircut, but I will also have hat hair.

21

Munich

The outcome of the haircut before Germany was crucial. I had to look good for Sabrina because she hadn't seen me in a couple months. My hair ended up being cut unevenly and too short. I was horrified. I went to the car, looked in the mirror and realized how royally screwed up it was. I went back in and asked someone to fix it but she made it worse! I spent the next week obsessing over it. I woke up each day analyzing how much more hair grew back. I was so nervous that Sabrina wouldn't be attracted to me when I got there.

On my last Friday at work I picked up my paycheck and left Tampa to move my stuff back to Miami. Tampa turned out to be a failed experiment. After moving everything back to Miami I flew to Munich. I tried so hard to look good for Sabrina. I ate small meals leading up to the trip and barely ate anything on the plane so my body looked better when I saw her. I couldn't believe how nervous I was. She picked me up at the airport and I was impressed she could drive a manual transmission. Driving through Germany with my foreign girlfriend made me feel really cool. We arrived at her studio apartment and caught up. The previous week before I came was the only week we didn't spend a lot of time on the phone. I figured it was because we were about to see each other. The first night Sabrina said she had to make a phone call to a girlfriend of hers. She was outside the apartment talking and I was almost positive I heard a man's voice on the other end of the phone. The next night she received a text message from someone just before midnight. She read it with a smirk on her face but didn't say who it was. While she was in the bathroom my curiosity got the best of me and I saw it was sent from a man named Florian. The text was in German and had a smiley face at the end. I checked her phone history from the day before and Florian was on the phone with her when she claimed to be talking to that girlfriend. I didn't know if she was cheating, but I confronted her about the lie. Her face turned bright red and she was speechless. I took her cell phone in the bathroom, locked the door, and told her I wanted to read the text messages. I didn't speak German so I had no idea what they said. After she pleaded for a while that I not read the messages, I exited the bathroom and told her I wanted to break up. There was no way we would have ever worked out anyway. She was going to live in Germany. I was never going to move there. We had a big argument and I could tell she felt really bad about lying to me. During that first week she went to work during the day and I would spend inordinate amounts of time looking at myself in the mirror. I thought that if I was better looking she would have never risked talking to other guys. She would have probably tried to stay in Miami that summer if I was really attractive. I decided that she must have dated me because she was lonely at school and was just waiting to find someone better back home. I still wasn't positive that she cheated on me, but was really upset with her for lying and could only assume the worst. I decided I would stay for the first week and weekend and try to make the best of my visit. Then on the following Monday I would visit Nick in Nice, France where he was at the time. I couldn't bear the thought of having to spend another five weekdays sitting in her apartment looking in the mirror wondering why I wasn't good enough for her while she was at work. We somehow managed to have an enjoyable weekend. We drove through villages to Neuschwanstein castle and the views were unbelievable. We took a bunch of pictures at the top while overlooking the region and I never posted any on Facebook because I hated the way I looked.

After the weekend I was ready to get away from the constant reminder of my inadequacy. On Monday morning I was relying on her alarm to wake me up since I didn't have an international cell phone. Somehow I slept through the alarm and woke up with only 15 minutes to get to the train. I threw together my bag and sprinted through Munich to the train station. When I was half way there I decided to check my pocket for the train ticket. It wasn't there. I realized it was still in Sabrina's purse. I stopped in my tracks, slumped my shoulders and started walking back to her apartment. I knew her apartment was on the 2nd floor but couldn't remember which number it was when I looked at the buzzers. I didn't want to ring everyone's bell at 7:15 in the morning. I ended up seeing a woman walking around on a first floor apartment. I knocked on the window and pointed to the door. She said something in German kind of yelling at me. I didn't understand, but she buzzed me in. I found the apartment on the 2nd floor and my now ex- girlfriend, thinking I wouldn't be back until Friday, was surprised to see me. I explained what happened- suspecting she never set the alarm and knew she had my ticket the whole time. I ended up having to go through another brutal week of being alone during the days and analyzing everything about my appearance. We kind of acted like we were dating the entire time much like when Laura visited during spring break in Miami after our breakup freshman year. I seemed to be developing a knack for getting myself into these awkward situations. Luckily, the rest of the week wasn't terrible. Finally, Sunday arrived and Sabrina drove me to the airport. We got there and it was time to say goodbye. She came in and we were standing next to the terminal after I checked my bag. We had a good-luck-in-life talk accompanied by a kiss goodbye. I went through the terminal and to my consternation nobody was waiting in the area by my plane. And the plane was gone! I found out it took off a few minutes early and they had paged me, but we never heard them call my name since we were outside of the terminal. This was turning into a disastrous trip. I had to stay yet another day with the girl who lied to me and made me feel worthless. After calling Sabrina's cell phone from the airport and having her come back to pick me up, I was sure I would never make it out of Germany. Thankfully, I was able to schedule a flight the next day and ultimately did make it out of there emotionally wounded.

I ended up traveling 30 hours door to door on four different flights the next day to Maine, the only place that could cheer me up. I didn't have pain from the heartbreak like I did with Laura, my first love. I might have been in denial a little, but I believe I knew deep down Sabrina wasn't the right girl for me. Also, I now realized I had made some meaningful progress in counseling. My brother didn't have a girlfriend there that year which helped me feel less alone. We took a flight on a small sea plane one day over the lake and I took photos inside the plane with my brother-in-law. I didn't like the way I looked in the pictures. They were some of the greatest shots and I couldn't post them on Facebook yet again.

22

Alone in the Real World

Now I had to go back to Miami without school, without a career lined up, and no free counselor to see every week through school anymore. But I did have a magnificent view outside my floor to ceiling glass windows and wraparound balcony of the clear blue water in Biscayne Bay and South Beach. I never got tired of that view.

I took a job in finance at a small start-up company in Brickell, which was the financial district of Miami. There was a magazine on the front desk for people in the waiting area which had a close up picture of Chris Martin from Coldplay on the cover. People had recently told me that I looked like him. I hated being told I looked like any celebrity because I knew I didn't. At best I was an ugly version of them with a slight resemblance. I used to see that magazine cover every day with his perfect skin when I walked in and wished that I looked exactly like him.

That company was selling oil and gas drilling investments in Texas. When the price of oil dropped in the fall of 2008 the company disbanded. I had a couple jobs during this year and really didn't know what I wanted to do with my life. I was 23 with a degree in International Finance and Marketing and with no real interest in the financial world. I wanted to do something real. I wanted to make some kind of a difference, but was facing the reality of bills and student loans for the first time.

During this first year out of college I realized that counseling had definitely helped because I became less obsessed with my appearance. I was more aware of the thoughts and ways to counteract them. From sessions with Stacy I learned I didn't have to entertain the thoughts when they came in. She had me practice blocking off a small amount of time in my day where I allowed myself to think about my appearance. If a thought popped up outside of that time, I could say, "No, I don't have to think about this now. I will think about this tonight for 10 minutes, but now is time to work." I also would randomly make lists of things I was thankful for in my life. With gratitude, it was harder to feel sorry for myself. But no matter how strong I felt, I always knew I was one really bad comment or haircut away from falling apart. And that's exactly what happened. I thought I had figured out a good haircut that minimized my ugliness for the 20th time in my life. I couldn't trust barbers though, so I tried cutting it myself. I accidentally knocked the clip off the razor and took a chunk of hair off. I was devastated. I tried to fix it by taking a little off on each side. I couldn't get it right. I decided I was at the point of no return and shaved my head. I walked out of the bathroom and looked like a skin head. I shaved my head exactly three times in my life and greatly regretted it each time. I went out to a party with friends that night and could feel people staring at me. I saw an old acquaintance from school and she only talked to me for a minute and then walked away quickly. I realized I looked scary. All the work I had done on my thinking and anything I felt good about had been undone.

I had recently found another sales job on Craigslist in an office in South Beach. Scared to show my shaved head to anyone else, I arrived at work with a hat on and luckily my boss was OK with me wearing it. This particular job had an office that was connected to a hotel with a pool in Miami Beach right off the famous Lincoln Road. I would leave the office and go to the bathroom intended for the hotel guests at the pool out back. I would go out there for 10 or 15 minutes at a time, take my hat off and just stare at my ugly head. After a month and a half I took my hat off in the office and one of my coworkers told me I looked funny without it on.

I had a lot of anxiety when friends from New Jersey visited because I didn't feel like I could show them a fun time. I had increasingly become a loner and had very little in the way of a social life. Luckily, Memo was incredibly good at entertaining people and would always help me out. My hometown friend since 3rd grade, Steve, visited while my head was still shaved. Steve was shy when we were younger but had been pretty successful with dating girls during college. He had a great deal of confidence after college. I felt like he always had an image of me being confident and good at talking to girls. That's how he remembered me in middle school when I dated Jen, the prettiest girl in our grade. He never seemed to change his impression. It was a lot to live up to when I saw him. I didn't want to lose this image. It was nice to pretend that I was the confident person he thought I was. But it was especially difficult to maintain this façade when I felt truly hideous. Steve mentioned how a pickup line he used on a girl was that he had a great hairline and his grandfather still had a full head of hair. He pulled his hair back for the girl and said he would never go bald. I started fearing going bald. What would life be like when I got older if I lost my hair? Would I constantly feel as ugly as I did with a shaved head? I wore a hat the entire time and survived Steve's visit. He didn't seem to lose the image he had of me.

I started taking vitamins that I read can make your hair grow back quicker. I would have done anything to get back to my normal state of ugliness instead of this complete repulsiveness. I was truly unbearable to look at. My hair did eventually grow back in and I was relieved when it finally did. I made a pact with myself to never cut my own hair again.

My brother and his two friends visited for New Year's Eve while Memo and Nick were back overseas. It was scary to have to entertain the three of them alone. I was able to bring them to Key Largo and Jim saved me by bringing us out on his boat. My brother was attending law school in Boston and recently started dating another student who happened to be from South Florida. She came out on the boat with us in the Keys. I caught her staring at me and wondered if she was thinking about how ugly I was compared to my brother.

Another night I tried bringing my brother and his two friends to South Beach, but I just wasn't much of a partier. We went to Mangos Tropical Café in South Beach which is a famous restaurant that turns into a club at night. I tried dancing and losing my inhibitions but felt like a huge loser. I wanted my brother to think I had a great life down there and was a really happy person. After their visit I realized the only joy I had in my life was with my roommates. I love them to death and if not for them and the great people I met in Miami I'm convinced I would have entered full blown depression. I never felt comfortable hanging out with people who only cared about partying. I liked having real friends who just liked me for me.

This was now my 5th year living with Nick and Memo. We lived on the same floor in the dorms freshman year, spent three years in our off campus house, and now lived in the high rise apartment. They practically knew me better than I knew myself. I can count to this day on one hand the number of people I truly let in on how obsessed I was with thoughts regarding my appearance. But looking back, my best friends knew without being told. Memo once made a comment that I wasn't the most confident guy. He had a lot of success in dating which he credited to his confidence. He was trying to tell me that confidence was the most important aspect in attracting a partner. He wasn't trying to be demeaning when saying I lacked it, but he was right. All my close friends were aware. Nick and Memo certainly knew. They knew that I would sometimes isolate myself in my room because female friends were coming over. With all the time we spent together, they were bound to figure it out. They caught me spending too much time in the bathroom in front of the mirror. They picked up on my self-defeating comments. I think it's like when an addict thinks nobody knows about their addiction only to find out everyone is relieved they are seeking help when they confess. My closest friends, who I lived with during my darkest times in Miami, will nod their heads when they read this.

23

Back to School and Counseling

The office job in South Beach didn't really give me any hope for advancement in the future. I was now 24 and unhappy with my career prospects so I chose to go back to school. I decided getting a 2nd degree in accounting could help me. Part of the reason I went back to school was because the job market wasn't great and I figured having another degree would help my prospects. Looking back this was probably a big mistake because I took out a lot of student loans to fund my schooling. I don't know why I chose a major that would involve doing a lot of work alone in the real world with the potential for even further isolation.

I left my job and went back to school full time at the University of Miami. I was excited to become reacquainted with every mirror on campus that I had become so familiar with in the past. I guess I didn't learn my lesson the first time about making grades the primary source of my self-worth. I dove right in the first weekend secluding myself from friends and spending the entire weekend in the library. I learned that big accounting firms wanted people with high GPA's so it was the perfect excuse to obsess over school again and lose all balance in my life. The one really good decision I made was going back to the counseling center. I once again set up weekly sessions to talk about my appearance related issues. With my hair grown back in, I felt like I was in a slightly better place than two years ago at my first counseling session when I had no place to turn. I was still very aware that I recently had a complete meltdown over my bad haircut debacle. Part of the reason I went to therapy this time was to see if I could figure out a way to truly not care about my looks at all other than just being clean and presentable to society. I wanted to see if I could actually have a bad haircut, an acne breakout, or my shirt off in front of strangers or my best friends and really not care. Losing my preoccupations in those scenarios seemed like a wildly unattainable goal, but I really wanted to know if I could get there. I met my new counselor, Donna, and explained to her my reasons for coming back to counseling. She read over my file from 2008 with Stacy before our first session.

"Now I know you covered a lot of topics with Stacy a couple years ago. What would you like to talk about today?"

"I realized one of my biggest problems is that I am always comparing my looks to other people. Whether it's at the gym, hanging out with friends, or in class, it is incessant. I just want it to end. "

"How does it make you feel when you see someone with a feature that you want?"

"Well I remember hearing in a psychology class that one of the main contributors to human's happiness is how we feel we are doing compared to those around us. For instance if we get better grades than our friends, we feel smart. Or if we have more money than our neighbors, we feel wealthy and are more likely to be content with our finances. So if I went to Harvard I might feel stupid because I would probably be at the bottom of the class. Or if I moved to Beverly Hills I might feel very poor because most people there have a lot more money than me. I understand this concept of comparison contributing to people's contentment. In other areas of my life I feel like I am good at not deriving my happiness or contentment from comparison to people around me. But when it comes to my appearance, it seems like all I do is compare myself to others and let it bring me down. Jealousy and inadequacy are my overwhelming feelings in these situations."

"And you think most people around you are more attractive than you?"

"Yes. Well the funny thing is when I walk around campus or anywhere I tend to focus on people that have what I think are the least amount of flaws. Sometimes when I'm thinking somewhat rationally I will realize that everyone has flaws. Once in awhile I will see someone with a defect that I have and wonder how much they think about it. I wonder how much it affects their life. I usually assume there is no way they obsess over it the way I do. But usually I tend to focus on the most attractive person and wish I looked like them. I can walk by 20 people all with different body shapes and faces and I will zero in the best looking one and wonder why I can't look like them. I will think how much better my life would be if I looked like them."

"Tell me more about what goes through your head when you see someone that you think does have some flaws, someone that doesn't look how you want to look."

"If I see someone who does have noticeable flaws I will actually usually be jealous of them because they don't seem to care. It wasn't always this way. For so many years I wanted to be perfect and figured most people with flaws felt the way I did. I wanted a perfect body, face, hair, smile, skin tone, height, eyes, head shape and size. Perfect everything. But now when I see people with flaws I think I would settle for being someone who just doesn't care. It seems most people aren't visibly affected by their flaws. They are able to socialize, smile, laugh and I don't get it. I don't get how they just don't care. I mean they must care to some extent. But it doesn't seem to stop them from being able to live a normal life. I'm here because I want to learn if I too cannot care."

Donna made me feel comfortable. I was glad I had returned to weekly counseling. After the first session I determined I felt much more confident than two years ago. The desperation was thankfully gone. I'm guessing part of it was maturing. But make no mistake about it, if I got another really bad haircut, or had a serious acne breakout, I probably would have been too weak to handle it. With that realization, I did wonder if the preoccupations were something I would just have to live with my whole life, with the hope of diminishing the thoughts as much as possible. I figured I might just have to learn through therapy to train my brain not to go into serious mood swings every time I didn't like the way I looked in the mirror or a photo. But perhaps ultimately I'd have to accept that the thoughts would always be there.

This was a strange year for me. I felt like I was growing in many ways. Someone told me that my 20s should be for learning and growing and that's what they had been thus far. I was 24 years old and surrounded by students a couple years younger than me finishing up their first degree. I felt a little more secure than I did in the past. I didn't make many friends this time at school. I was there mainly for academic purposes. I joined the Accounting Honors Society and made a few acquaintances through that, but friendship wasn't my focus. I still did a lot of mirror checking, but the mood swings usually weren't as bad.

During the fall semester I did meet one girl in class named Madeline who I became friends with. In the beginning of our friendship we mostly talked about her problems and uncertainty with her career decisions.

We were sitting in my car making conversation one night and she said, "I feel like you know so much about me but I don't know you at all. Tell me about yourself." I went on to describe in detail my relationship with Laura throughout high school and the first couple years of college. I talked in detail about Sabrina and described our relationship. I then briefly filled in a few holes with school and my jobs. She thought it was really strange that I described who I was by my relationship history and reminded me about this several times throughout our friendship. I had become so obsessed with my relationships that I let them define who I was. I didn't feel all alone when I was dating someone. The relationships also validated my looks to some extent. I couldn't be *that* ugly if someone would date me. I eventually thought love was the cure all for everything. It was enlightening to have Madeline's observation make me realize I defined myself in an unhealthy manner. I knew I had a lot of work to do. I still didn't really know who I was.

One night towards the end of the fall semester I grabbed a snack at Whole Foods across from campus and was eating alone in my car in the parking garage. I saw a woman getting ready for what appeared to be a date, probably a first date. She had it. She had what I have. She fixed herself in the mirror for about 10 minutes, first the makeup, then the hair. Checking and rechecking, shaking her head in displeasure from time to time. She got out of the car and looked at her reflection in every car window to check if anything changed, to reassess her own fleeting approval perhaps. Who was she meeting? Did he care about her looks as much as she did? Would it ever work if he did? I just wanted to walk over to her and say, "It doesn't matter." I wanted to shake some sense into her and say, "Whoever you are going to meet doesn't care. He wants to like you as a person. He wants to enjoy his time with you. They will leave tonight caring more about how they enjoyed their time with you than your appearance. They want to know whether or not your values are aligned on big issues, deal breaker issues. Kids or no kids type things. They don't care if your hair is parted to your perfection. They don't care how you look in one type of lighting compared to another. And if they do care they're not the right person." I wanted to say all those things to her. It wouldn't have made a difference though. I've heard the logic. It makes sense momentarily. But the thoughts are too powerful. She probably would have looked at me like I was crazy even though it would have addressed all of her biggest fears and concerns about that date. Did she too look at magazines and watch TV shows as a child slowly developing an image of what she wanted to look like?

24

Acne Treatment

During final exam week in December I was studying in the library and started browsing the internet for ways to fix acne scarring. The scars on my back had bothered me since high school and I was curious if there had been any advances in the industry. I stumbled across an article on Msnbc.com about triplets who were badly burned in a house fire at only 17 months old. The three sisters, now 22, struggled to deal with the burns that covered up to 30% of their bodies for most of their lives. The sisters were from Texas and heard about a new innovative laser treatment for scars being performed by a dermatologist named Jill Waibel. I read on and saw Dr. Waibel was located in West Palm Beach, Fl. The treatment proved extremely effective on the girls and was considered a medical miracle. The best part was that the laser sessions were actually affordable. I called Dr. Waibel's office the next day and it just so happened that she recently moved her office from West Palm Beach to Miami only minutes from my school. I set up a consultation. When I met Dr. Waibel, she told me to take my shirt off for some pictures. After analyzing the scars, she told me I could expect a significant improvement over time with a series of laser treatments. I was extremely excited and couldn't wait to start. One of the lasers during the first treatment would turn my skin red and an outer layer of skin would actually peel off. I figured the timing was perfect because Memo and Nick would be back in Europe for the holidays and nobody would have to know about it. I arrived at her office a few weeks later and underwent the first treatment. The lasers weren't painful and the experience wasn't as bad as expected. I went home and saw I looked really red. Dr. Waibel told me the skin would gradually peel and the redness would disappear in less than a week.

I was still really red two days after the procedure and to my own surprise felt ready to take a big step. I decided to talk to a friend from school named Lindsay who I thought might also be struggling with appearance related thoughts based on some of our conversations. Lindsay was the only friend I met that semester other than Madeline. My counseling sessions with Donna had given me some confidence that I could open up to certain close friends without feeling judged. Despite feeling vulnerable with my red skin, it seemed like a perfect opportunity to finally open up to someone I could actually help. I really just wanted to talk about what had bothered me and see if Lindsay was able to relate at all. I had wished someone talked to me during my isolation. I asked her to meet up for a cup of coffee at Starbucks across from our campus.

"Hi Mark. How are you?"

I had already told her that my face was going to look funny from a treatment and not to be alarmed.

"Good. So do you notice anything different about me?"

"Yes. But I can't quite put my finger on it. Did you get a haircut?"

"Ha Ha. Well as I told you I had a treatment done. That is actually part of why I wanted to meet up with you. I just wanted to talk to someone about what I did because I haven't told anyone. You have to promise not to judge me though. And don't worry. My face won't be red forever. It will be normal in a few days"

"I promise I won't judge. So what kind of treatment did you have?"

"Well I had bad acne scars on my back and neck. I also had a few on my face. I found a dermatologist down here that has successfully experimented with a new treatment and I figured I'd give it a try. I have always hated my scars."

"Wow. I never even noticed you had any."

"I do a pretty good job of hiding them. If I ever take my shirt off I make sure people are standing in front of me. My issues with the scars have actually been really annoying. Every time I've gone to the beach or pool with people since high school I had to work hard to make sure they were standing in front of me the entire time."

"That sounds like a lot of work. I would have never guessed you struggled with something like that."

"Yea, well this is kind of hard for me to talk about because I've only told one friend in my life, but I actually have been seeing a counselor at school this year and saw a different one two years ago. It's not only my acne. I never felt like I fit in during high school or in Miami and have struggled with so many issues about my appearance for many years. I didn't tell you this but I was in the fraternity Pike my freshman and sophomore year, you know the jock frat. I didn't want you to think I was a jerk because I know they have a bad reputation."

"Wait a second. *You* were in Pike? I'm sorry, can we get the check? I didn't realize how late it is."

"Lindsay, I wasn't really a Pike. Nobody could ever believe I was in that fraternity when they met me. They always said you seem too nice to be a Pike. What they really meant was I didn't seem cocky enough to be a Pike. But seriously they weren't bad guys. Everything you heard is just rumors."

"I know, I'm kidding! Mark, I really respect you for opening up to me. I actually have been seeing a counselor for a couple of years for self esteem issues and other things that have bothered me."

"Really? I have found the counseling extremely helpful. Sometimes it isn't even the advice or revelations that really make a difference. It's often just the act of getting my thoughts and concerns out that makes me feel better. The more I hold onto my thoughts, the more power they seem to have."

"Yes! I know exactly what you are talking about. Counseling has helped me through some really difficult times."

"I don't know why, but I felt comfortable opening up to you. I feel like most people would think I am superficial if I told them how much I think about my appearance."

"I know you're not like that. I understand what you are going through. If you ever want to talk more about any issues you are having, feel free to reach out to me."

"Thanks. That means a lot to me."

I drove home and thought about my conversation with Linsday. I felt such a deep connection with her while we talked that night. For a moment it felt like struggling with my obsessive thoughts was OK. I didn't feel so alone.

25

Final Months in Miami

School started up again in the spring and I determined I was ready to move back home after finals in May. I had been going back and forth in my head for the last three or four years about where I wanted to live in my 20s. Each year I would decide I was going to move home, then visit New Jersey in November or December, feel the freezing temperature and quickly remember the warm winter sun in South Florida. Previously I thought I couldn't ever leave Florida because I looked so much better tan. It was normal to be tan in Florida. If I moved back to New Jersey and used tanning beds again everyone would know about my insecurities. But at this point I had accepted I couldn't always be tan and would have to deal with being pale. I actually had already started spending a lot less time in the sun after visiting a dermatologist and having a potentially cancerous mole removed. I was finally ready to make the move. I just needed a job. I had taken out a bunch of student loans, put forth a lot of effort into school and didn't want to come up empty handed. I didn't make wise decisions earlier in college like others who got internships. Most of the people who had internships were much more successful in the job search process.

I met a recruiter at a career fair on campus that spring who forwarded my resume up north to their New York

City office. The company was Marcum, a rapidly growing accounting firm. I ended up getting a call on St. Patrick's Day but didn't answer the phone in time. I heard the voicemail from Marcum's human resources representative expressing interest and spent the next two weeks trying to get in touch with her. When I finally did, she told me I could interview in May when I got back from school. I was scared the position would be filled by then. I quickly remembered I was flying home in two weeks and asked if I could interview sooner and they agreed. I flew home to New Jersey and stayed at my sister's apartment across the river from New York City the night before the interview.

I woke up and looked at myself in the mirror. I still hated the way I looked when I woke up. My hair looked funny and I would always wonder if a woman could really be attracted to me after seeing my appearance in the morning. I took a shower and tried to clear my mind for the big day. I fixed myself up in the bathroom for a few more minutes before leaving for the train to New York. I was very nervous but decided to go in as confidently as I possibly could. I was terrified that they would ask me technical questions. I walked down the streets of the city and tried hard not to play the eye contact game with each passerby. I didn't want to deflate my confidence. I went to the front desk where they took my picture and provided a guest sticker. I didn't like the way I looked in the picture but fought off negative thoughts. I rode the elevator up 12 floors and checked in at the reception. It was a fancy lobby with a flat screen TV. They told me the HR contact I had been in touch with wasn't in today. My heart was beating really fast and they said another HR rep would interview me. I talked to the woman they set me up with for 15 minutes and the conversation went well. I think she was just making sure I wasn't crazy or anything. She said that since I flew up, there would be no follow up interview and the entire process would be conducted that day. They walked me upstairs to the office of the managing partner of the entire NYC office. My heart was pounding harder than it ever had before and I was sweating under my suit. I wondered if he would judge me by my appearance and hoped he didn't think I was too ugly to work there. We talked and he didn't ask me any technical questions. It went really well. He told me that he assumed I would be fielding offers from other companies so they would be very pleased if I chose Marcum. I was shocked. He basically gave me an offer on the spot and I walked out of there with an incredible high.

I walked down the street beaming with confidence. I didn't care how attractive or unattractive I was. I felt like every girl I walked by was looking at me as I stood tall for one of the first times in years. All of my hard work had paid off. Sitting in the library alone until midnight with the constant torment of my thoughts wasn't a total waste. Staying at home and studying when my friends all went out was the right thing to do after all even though I only studied for a fraction of the time. I didn't regret all of the fun times I had missed out on anymore. None of that mattered now because I had a job offer with a starting salary of $58,000 awaiting and a new life in New York City.

Back in Miami the last few weeks of school flew by and I had to face the fact that I would be losing Donna from my life. I had been seeing her weekly for the entire school year.

"So Donna, I guess this is it. This is our last session."

"It is Mark. We've come a long way."

"I know. I'm glad we met. I laughed with you. I cried with you. And I think I grew with you."

"You were brave in our sessions. You went to uncomfortable places. I know it sometimes got worse before it got better after some of our deep introspection."

"I know. You often pointed out that I would laugh or change the subject when we got too deep. But eventually I was willing to go to those uncomfortable places. I had to."

"What are your thoughts on moving back home without counseling? Are you going to use some of the techniques we worked on?"

"I think I will do alright. I am a little nervous, but I'm not that scared. I survived the month of winter break without seeing you and I think I made a lot more progress. I will definitely continue to practice some things we worked on."

"OK good. I think you will do just fine. Keep doing things you are passionate about like we talked about. Your passions will help you maintain that purpose in life that you always talked about."

"I will. And I really want to thank you. I know you work very hard and some of your subjects can be very frustrating, like yours truly for example. I want to let you know that you made a serious impact on my life. You must know how big of a difference you have made. Thank you for everything, Donna."

"Mark, it was my pleasure. I appreciate your honesty throughout our sessions. I wish you success and if things get tough, don't be afraid to find another counselor up in New Jersey. You may find that helpful, even if the sessions are more for maintenance."

I left Donna's office and felt really good about my time with her. In some ways she knew me better than anyone I ever met. Only Donna and my first counselor Stacy truly knew the thoughts that dominated my mind. I said my goodbyes to everyone else who was left in South Florida. I drove around on a nostalgic ride looking at all of the places where I had so many memories. The freshman dorms with all of my struggles, my fraternity house where I never felt like I fit in, my house off campus with my best friends where I had so many good times but also became depressed, the counseling center where I started learning how to deal with my issues, the beach where I could never feel comfortable with my shirt off, and my condo in downtown Miami where I finally started living without constant obsessive thoughts. I had been through so much in this city. My parents had dropped me off at the edge of campus and said goodbye seven years earlier. My father who rarely got emotional or said anything sentimental said, "Mark, be careful. There are a lot of women in Miami." My mom cried because she thought I would never move back to New Jersey and she was almost right. It was very hard to move back. This city, with its love for vanity, came very close to chewing me up and spitting me out. I fought back though and survived my experience there. I left with the city in my rear view mirror and ready to embark on a new life.

26

New York City

I moved back home and was ready to start with Marcum in New York City, the most hectic place I have ever been. Before starting at the New York City office, I had a two week long training in Long Island. I decided this was going to mark a new life for me. I was with all new people and none of them knew anything about me. Nobody in my life really knew how severe my insecurities were, but everyone who knew me was aware of my ability to isolate myself. These people knew nothing. I had a clean slate with them. I went into that training being the most outgoing person I could imagine. I pretended that I had no insecurities and it felt wonderful. People quickly came to know me as extremely friendly and talkative. A lot of the coworkers wanted to friend me on Facebook. I told them that I wouldn't accept anyone because a friend of mine had a bad experience at a previous employer. I didn't know what to tell them. If I was going to start a new life I couldn't have everyone judging me on all of my pictures from the past. One night we had a drink and appetizer party to meet all of the senior people we would be working with. I had been so good at socializing during the training because it was with all young people who were also nervous. I talked to the managing partner who had interviewed me about eight months ago and he didn't even seem to remember me. He must have been really busy the day we met or just didn't have a great memory. This was even more nerve racking. The guy who saw something in me and recommended Marcum hire me didn't even remember our interview!

The training ended and I was ready to start in my new office in New York City. The other people in my department throughout training were staying in Long Island or going to other offices. I was the only new one in New York City and was again scared. I got to the office and felt my confidence dwindling. A secretary walked me to a cubicle and I was all alone. Everyone was friendly, but I never felt totally comfortable there. I was now in a big city and barely knew anyone. I had grown apart from my childhood friends and started missing all my close college friends. Walking down the street in New York City was quite an experience for me. I would look at everyone and have many of those thoughts I had back on campus. I didn't have a counselor, but was doing better in one significant way. Despite the frequent trips to the bathroom, the mirror checking and constant comparing didn't seem to affect my self-worth as much as it did in the past. I could tell I had definitely made some progress but I wasn't a very good accountant. As a matter of fact, I was pretty bad because I had a lot of trouble focusing on my work. I wanted to do well so badly but couldn't handle the tremendous amount of autonomy. We were given projects and a projected budget of hours to complete them in which I had to manage all on my own. I had never learned how to concentrate very well at school. My obsessive thoughts still interfered greatly with my ability to work productively. I wasn't given ten hours to study in a library to complete three hours of work. There was one senior employee named Matty who I became close with. He shared some advice on several occasions. He was a very interesting guy and I really appreciated his outlook on life. Over lunch one day, I told Matty he seemed so comfortable in his own skin and he and made it clear he wasn't always that way. He told me that he used to be very nervous and unsure of himself but learned along the way to not take life so seriously. The only time I was really efficient was when I knew my job was truly on the line. I got word from another senior employee that I had to turn in a flawless project for the client I was working on. He said even then it might already be too late. I tried my best, but could tell based on feedback from the superior I was working for that I was in trouble. When the human resources representative and my boss told me it wasn't working out, I had already realized accounting wasn't right for me. There was no way I could handle a job like that, stuck with my own thoughts all day and minimal interaction with other people. I had been so productive at the restaurant in college because I had no other choice. If I wasn't efficient at Café Tu Tu Tango my boss, the cooks, and the customers waiting for their food would have all yelled at me. I couldn't simulate that pressure in accounting. I felt really stupid though because I had taken out a lot of student loans and spent the past year of my life working towards the CPA certification.

 I did some reflection and realized I was truly inspired by my two experiences with counseling now. I had sat across from my second counselor, Donna, on certain sessions and we connected on such a deep level. It was so much more real than any job I could imagine in the finance or accounting world. One of my final conversations with Donna in Miami last spring kept popping into my head. I told her some things that I was really passionate about. I told her that I had finally shared some of my obsessions with someone who I sensed was experiencing similar thoughts. I recalled the session:

"I am feeling conflicted about my future and wanted to talk about something a little different today."

"OK. What's on your mind?"

"I wanted to talk about some things regarding my future career path."

"OK. Like what?"

"Well I am really happy that I got a job in New York starting next year, but it's bothering me that I am going to be defined by being an accountant."

"What do you mean?"

"Well I am going to work a lot of hours at a desk in front of a computer. People are going to ask me what I do for a living and the answer will be accounting."

"Ok. So what's wrong with that? You aren't going to be solely defined by your job."

"I know. But I feel like there is going to be such a big difference between someone like me and you. I mean if someone asks me what I do for a living, I'm going to hate my answer. Someone once asked me what I want to do for a living and I said, "I dunno, something in business." He said, "OK. But what do you want to do that brings life to you?" I had no idea and it really made me think. I can tell *your* career brings life to you. I want my career to bring life to me. You feel good about what you do. You are making an impact. I know the world wouldn't work if everyone was a social worker or a volunteer, but my job is going to entail 60-70 hour weeks at times. I won't have any time or energy to do anything I'm passionate about."

"Well maybe at some point you can work at a less demanding company and find a balance. Also, people often switch jobs several times before they find the right career for them. Just because you are heading on this path now doesn't mean you will end up on that path permanently. It will all be part of your journey"

I hated her saying this. I always wanted everything planned out. I always wanted to know that I was on the right track and doing something that would make my life better in the future.

"I know. I didn't tell you this but I recently told my friend Lindsay about why I come to you. I had a feeling that she struggled like I do. I just felt so good telling her about all of my obsessions and issues. I could see her face and knew she had struggles like me. We connected in that moment. THAT brought life to me. I just want to make sure I don't get caught up living a life that doesn't bring life to me."

"Wow. I am impressed that you talked to Lindsay about your struggles. That shows some serious progress. I think the mere fact that you're aware you want to live a life that brings life to you will help ensure it happens. Why don't you try writing down something each day that you can do to bring life to you? Writing things down will help you keep them a priority."

With accounting not working out, it became evident I needed to change my path. I thought about that counseling session every day. I wanted to do something that brought life to me. Going back to school wasn't an option because I was in student loan debt up to my ears. My parents and siblings had already joked that I was a career student. I was seriously lacking a purpose in life and not sure what to do. I started reflecting on some things I learned in Miami.

27

What I learned

So what have I learned from all of my struggles? I learned that I needed help. I couldn't have effectively worked on my thinking alone. I went to the student counseling center in Miami out of desperation and it turned out to be the best decision I ever made. My initial counselor, Stacy, was the first person I told about my struggles. A tremendous weight was lifted off my shoulders after I opened up to her. My second counselor, Donna, helped me progress even further. We talked about more than my appearance struggles, and with her help I was able to open up to some of my closest friends about my obsessive thoughts. Opening up to friends was liberating and crucial for my growth.

Through counseling I learned I had no balance in my life. I became unhealthily focused on different aspects of life to create a distraction from the obsessive thoughts. I wanted to break the tie of self worth and my perception of my appearance. In an effort to do so, there were several external areas I tried to exclusively define myself by at different periods of high school and college.

Work/School

I mentioned that I did use work at the restaurant as a healthy distraction from my thoughts but I had to be careful. There were times when it wasn't even necessary to work at the restaurant, but I wanted to because work quieted my appearance thoughts. I would rather work than hang out with friends or even sit in class because it helped me forget about all my flaws. Defining myself by my performance in school alone was particularly dangerous because it tied in nicely with my appearance struggles. I placed unreasonable expectations on myself with grades just like with my desire to look perfect. Worse yet, I didn't have to see anyone when I was studying. An unhealthy obsession with grades gave me an excuse to isolate myself. I took away valuable opportunities to push my boundaries of comfort which were necessary to grow and fight my obsessive appearance thoughts.

Friends

My friends helped me so much in my life. When trying to break the tie of self-worth and my perception of my appearance, I did have to realize that I couldn't solely define myself by friends though. They had their own lives to live as well. Sometimes friends couldn't be there for reasons out of my control. Sometimes friends weren't who I thought they were. It was healthy for me to place a high level of importance on being a good friend and being there for people, but I had to make sure my happiness wasn't too linked to how many friends I had or how any particular friendship was going at a given time. I learned that friends do come and go throughout life. I have drifted apart from many friends because of distance and simply being in different stages of our lives. This doesn't mean I didn't learn from them and grow from the bonds I had with them. Also, the best friends I have made over the years will always be there for me if I ever need anything. And the same goes for me with them. If I hang out with my best friends, even without having seen them for years, it feels as if we never missed a beat. There are only a few friends that I have met like this and I truly do cherish those relationships. But the most important thing I have to realize is that friends are one piece of my life. They can't be everything, because when I lack a balance I become vulnerable to all of my appearance thoughts again.

Relationships

The most unhealthy area I exclusively defined myself by was my romantic relationships. When I went to a counselor freshman year after my first heartbreak with Laura, I explained how devastated I was. I said that I lost my identity and couldn't imagine going on living without her. I told him the thought of Laura with another person made me sick to my stomach. He said a lot of things but the one thing he said which really stuck with me was, "It's OK. Haven't you ever thought that you will fall in and out of love several times in your life? This is your first experience with love and you are going to grow from this. You will eventually learn to make a relationship one component of a balanced life." It seemed so simple, but for days I thought, "No. What is he talking about? Laura is the girl I was going to marry. I don't want to fall in and out of love several times in my life. I can't go through heartbreak several times or even one more time. She was my entire life." Well the counselor was right. I have fallen in and out of love several times. I have learned more about myself and what I am ultimately looking for in a partner each time. Moving on from relationships has been trying, but he spoke from experience. Most people don't marry the first person they date. I didn't want to believe this. I wanted to believe that I was different from everyone else. Also, I was too scared to be alone. The main reason I was devastated for months was because I had lost my identity in that relationship. My entire self-worth was being generated from my involvement with Laura. Considering my vulnerability to negative appearance based thoughts, I had set myself up for a miserable recovery by solely defining myself by the relationship. My entire happiness was related to how things were going between us. If we got into an argument I would be so upset that it would ruin my whole day. I had nothing else going on in my life. In my head the only thing that mattered was how we were doing as a couple. Just like how I felt when all of my happiness was tied to my perception of my appearance, all of my emotional well being was tied to my relationship.

****

I learned that work, school, friends, and relationships all needed to be pieces of a balanced life. I also determined I could benefit from finding a purpose. It didn't have to be saving the world. My purpose just needed to be something positive and healthy. My only purpose had been to find a way to look good and in turn feel good. Once achieved, then and only then could I worry about the other aspects of life. People with a purpose seemed to obtain very little of their self-worth and confidence from their perception of their appearance. Sure, nobody wants to look like an alien. A little of any normal person's self-worth comes from presenting their outward appearance in a fashion acceptable to themselves and others. But for people with a purpose, looks weren't their dominant thought when out in public. Yes, most normal people do a quick check in the bathroom mirror. Five maybe ten seconds. Nothing in the teeth: check. Hair isn't all over the place: check. OK back out to socialize. How did they do it? How did they resist staying in front of the mirror and thoroughly analyzing themselves? Why didn't they stay in the bathroom looking at the mirror until someone else walked in or until people would start to wonder why they were gone so long? They were somehow able to avoid making their looks the main focus of their thoughts.

Most importantly, I learned that I could live without the constant torment of thoughts about my appearance. There was a long period of time where I thought the incessant thoughts would be a lifelong struggle. Today, I am proud to say that through counseling and hard work, I have regained control of my life. I haven't completely arrested the thoughts and excessive mirror checking, but the huge emotional swings are rare.

With all the progress I made, I realized it was time to find a purpose. I decided my purpose at this point would be to help people who were struggling with the problems I had. The realization of how much time and energy I had wasted on my thoughts about appearance was becoming difficult to swallow. I was living with the guilt of missed opportunities. I could no longer keep this all bottled up. I knew I had a story to tell. I wasn't proud of it, but I looked around and knew I was not alone. I saw people every day that must have been going through what I went through. I used to think I was the only one. No matter how alone I had felt at so many times in my life, I now refused to believe I was the only one who generated a substantial amount of my self-worth from the perception of my appearance. Hollywood, television, movies, advertisements- there's no way I was the only one who was sold on life being better and easier if only I was more attractive. I didn't claim to have all of the answers on how to change this thinking. I might not have even had any. But one thing I knew for sure was that I wished I had someone to talk to throughout my struggles. Finally telling someone had made the thoughts less powerful. When I did open up, I had no longer felt alone.

I determined that writing would be the most effective method to share my experiences. With the encouragement of my counselors, I had done a little writing throughout college about my obsessive thoughts. My minimal experiences with writing helped put the irrational thoughts into perspective. I mentioned to Donna I wanted to write a book about my struggles during one of our sessions back in college. I thought a book in some ways could represent my victory over my obsession. At that time I knew completing a book was unlikely because I rarely followed through with any goals.

But now, with the benefit of some serious reflection, I had an overwhelming desire to start the book. I brought my laptop to a Barnes & Noble coffee shop and started typing. Just when I started writing about the earliest experiences I could remember, two guys walked up to the Starbucks counter that looked like models. They were both with pretty girls. All four of them had characteristics that I always wanted. Their bodies were perfect. Their faces were attractive. They had perfect hair and seemed very confident. Life must have been so easy for them. They didn't have to worry about the things I did. They didn't have trouble sleeping at night due to thoughts about their imperfections. They didn't have mood swings when they went to the bathroom. They didn't know about the emotional rollercoaster of being unattractive. They didn't know how damaging a comment about one's appearance could be to their psyche. People called them hot. People talked to them simply because they were attractive. They could easily make eye contact during conversations. Seeing them got my mind racing with all the thoughts that plagued me for years. After an hour of typing, someone glanced over at my computer screen, then quickly looked away. It made me feel uncomfortable and I started typing about the experience:

I have every intention of allowing people to read this, but still feel very uneasy when I think someone can see over my shoulder as I type. This is a window to my soul. This is a look at the painful life and torment I have endured. It is quite embarrassing. I didn't have terrible things happen to me. I wasn't born an orphan. I'm not a victim of tragic circumstances. My problems are all in my head, self created. No, I didn't ask for them. I wished the thoughts to go away millions of times. But in the end they were my own thoughts. Not external circumstances beyond my control. So yes, it is scary to think someone can get a glimpse inside my head.

The End

Bibliography

ANNE E. BECKER, R.A. (2002). Eating behaviours and attitudes following prolonged exposure to television among ethnic Fijian adolescent girls. *The British Journal of Psychiatry,* 180:509-514

A special thanks to The British Journal of Psychiatry and Dr. Anne E. Becker for granting permission of the use of this study.

Resources

- National Suicide Prevention Hotline:

  1.800.273.TALK (8255)

- www.SuicidePreventionLifeline.org

- National Institute of Mental Health (NIMH)

  www.nimh.nih.gov

- Substance Abuse and Mental Health Services

  Administration (SAMHSA) www.samhsa.gov

- http://en.wikipedia.org/wiki/Body_dysmorphic

  _disorder

Printed in Great Britain
by Amazon